WITNESS AND WORK

RESOURCES

Witness and Work *RESOURCES*

Brian Allenby

Terra Nova Publications

First published by Terra Nova Publications Ltd, 2004

*Published in Great Britain by
Terra Nova Publications Ltd
PO Box 2400, Bradford on Avon, Wiltshire BA15 2YN*

Cover design by Gazelle Creative Productions Ltd.

ISBN 1 90194 930 3

*Printed in Great Britain
by Bookmarque Ltd, Croydon*

Contents

Introduction

I remember, as a teenager, foolishly riding my bicycle from my home in Leeds to Malham in the Yorkshire Dales, a journey of about forty miles. It was a Friday afternoon and I and a friend intended to spend the weekend in the Dales between Malham, at the head of the Aire valley, and Kettlewell in upper Wharfedale. We arrived at the youth hostel in Malham at around 8.00 p.m., to find that it was fully booked. The warden said that there was room at Linton, near Grassington, which was about ten miles away, but we had to be there before 10.30 p.m. It was not an impossible journey provided that we had a map. We had both stayed at Linton before, so we knew that we had to travel back about five miles toward Skipton and then find the turn to Grassington, which should lead us toward Linton; simple for anybody who could read a map. Oh, he did mention a map —well, the truth was that neither of us had brought our OS map, but being typical teenagers we were both utterly confident that we could find our way. To cut a long story short, we arrived at Linton before

10.30 a.m. the following morning, somewhat tired and bedraggled, having slept in a hedge near the village of Thorpe, just two miles from Linton!

It really is easy to get lost if you lack the right tools to navigate your journey, and being a Christian at work can be a little like that too, especially when, in spiritual terms, you are in an alien environment. It is not easy to be a Christian in the twenty–first century workplace; it never has been easy, at any time. For over sixty years, the organisation *Christians at Work* has been seeking to encourage, support and equip Christian people for workplace witness and evangelism, and during that time it has produced a number of resource papers aimed at helping working Christian people to come to terms with their situation at work. These papers deal with the real day to day issues: how to find other Christians; how to form a fellowship group; special event opportunities and group programmes, etc. What we have tried to do here is to bring together all of our resource papers, revised and edited, to form a single volume of resources and helps. They are not exhaustive, but they have been reviewed and updated over the years and new sections added from time to time. We have also tested the usefulness of these resources by asking our groups to give us feedback when appropriate. I hope that you find the information useful and encouraging, and if you do not find help you need here, contact us directly and we will do our best to put you on the right track.

A lot of the work here was undertaken by my two predecessors at *Christians at Work*, Rod Baddams and Mark McConnell. I also believe that some of the information came about as a result of papers presented by invited guests at various CaW conferences and seminars and I am truly grateful for this. I have revised and edited most of the papers and added three more, but I must also acknowledge the input from my publisher who has assisted me with the further editing and also made very useful revision comments.

Again, this book is dedicated to all the many members, friends and supporters of the organisation and charity *Christians at Work*, especially those who labour day by day to live out their faith in the mission field that we call work.

Brian Allenby

1

STARTING A WORKPLACE CHRISTIAN FELLOWSHIP GROUP

This section contains a number of practical suggestions connected with the setting up of a workplace Christian Fellowship group. However, it does not pretend to be exhaustive. It offers *one* route to the formation of a CF group at work, and we are sure that some of the information in this chapter will be of help even to those who adopt a slightly different approach at the launch of their particular group.

FIRST STEPS

1. If more than one Christian is already keen to start a Christian Fellowship (CF) at work, meet together at lunchtime or after work to pray about it, seeking the Lord's wisdom and leading. (If you are the only one with the idea at present, approach personally one or two like-minded Christians at your workplace.) Above all else, pray!

2. Talk together about your vision and aims for a group. Do you share the same salvation by grace through faith in Jesus Christ? Do you have similar goals? Do you see the usefulness of a CF group at work in terms of encouragement to Christians, outreach to non–Christians, or both?

Thinking through those questions now will avoid confusion, and will also give you a definite challenge to present to the other Christians in your workplace. Some will need that —life is busy, and something vague and uncertain will not win them over.

3. List all the Christians you know in your workplace. Consider how to approach them (i.e. by email, letter or personally). If you know five Christians, it is probably better to see each of them personally. If there are ten or more, then because of the time involved it may be more realistic to email or send a letter.

If you mail, avoid making it an invitation to a meeting to discuss the start of a CF group. Some would not be able to attend, and would feel left out. Instead, make it a letter outlining your aims, and asking for their prayers, and for their written reactions to your ideas, by a given date. This will compel them to study the proposal. Chase up those who do not reply.

FURTHER PRELIMINARIES

Take time to consider the response to your conversations or letters. The general reaction may be that it is a good idea, but.... "But don't make me a leader," or, "But I'm very busy with all kinds of other commitments." Do not be put off by these reactions. If there were not some reservations about the idea, a CF group would probably have started long before this! To counter these hesitations, attention should be given to three questions that may already have been raised in the replies:

1. *What is a workplace Christian Fellowship group for?*
There are really two parallel aims: to provide encouragement and mutual support for Christians in the workplace, and to be a platform for witness to non–Christian colleagues.

2. *What kind of framework do we need to achieve these aims?*
The basic framework of a CF group is a regular meeting, plus a range of other specific activities or witness ventures that are not meeting–based. Meetings are important and to be encouraged. But we must not limit our thinking to meetings only. There is much other useful work a CF can do, which can involve people who find it difficult or impossible to get to meetings. If you have a company intranet, seek permission to use it and perhaps advertise your events; if people have access to the internet, or email facilities, this is an effective means of keeping in contact.

3. *What demands will a CF group make on the individual Christians?*
Involvement in a CF group need not be a huge time commitment. CF groups should be run so as not to put great time burdens on any one person. CF activities should not often encroach into evenings or weekends. On the other hand, even busy Christians (which should be all of them!) ought not to excuse themselves from CF group involvement simply because they are too busy to attend many meetings.

Even if an individual Christian works through lunch every day, there are still aspects of the CF group's overall work open to them, such as: praying; putting up notices; sending out emails, etc.

PREPARING FOR LAUNCH

At this stage you could issue a progress report to all the Christians at work. Attention will then turn to practicalities, and beneath each of the following questions, we give our own suggestions.

1. *How frequently are you going to meet?*
Most groups meet once a week, with twice a week, once a fortnight and once a month being the next most common frequencies. Those meeting twice a week usually devote one meeting to prayer and the other to Bible study, or have a guest speaker.

2. *At what time of the day are you going to meet?*
Most CF groups meet at lunchtime for half–an–hour. The advantage of this, compared with meeting after work, is that regular transport arrangements and evening commitments are not threatened, and outsiders are more likely to come. Whenever you meet, keep rigidly to advertised timings, avoiding late starts and finishes. If timings are seen to be reliable, people will be more willing to attend.

3. *Where are you going to meet?*
Off–site meetings have some minor advantages, but for relevance, economy of time and the likelihood of outsiders attending, an on–site venue is preferable, if a room is available. A regular booking of the same room is the ideal, but if this is not possible you may have to use a variety of venues, and devise a way of letting everyone know, possibly at short notice.

It is necessary and right to seek the permission of your management for the CF group to exist, to be known by the company name, and to use meeting rooms on work premises. In the vast majority of cases permission will be granted. Most companies have encountered CF groups before. Some will be encouraging and helpful; others will merely give permission and leave you to your own devices. This may be a good time to contact *Christians at Work,* whether or not your CF group intends to affiliate. *Christians at Work* has in the past helped to convince companies that CF groups are neither rare nor harmful!

4. *What sort of programme are you going to follow?*
There are two programmes that will need to work in parallel: a meetings programme and one for your other activities. We suggest that you start your meetings programme with a monthly cycle of weekly meetings, without any invited speakers or special meetings, and probably without any general publicity on notice boards. A modest beginning is always best —never launch out at a pace you cannot keep up. The following is a simple cycle that you may want to adopt or adapt:

- Week One: shared Bible study. Choose passage beforehand.
- Week Two: share testimonies —arrange for one or two in advance.
- Week Three: time of prayer.
- Week Four: well–led discussion on a relevant, planned topic.
- Week Five (if any): further time of prayer.

After two months or so, you will probably want to change this cycle, to incorporate a better–planned series of useful Bible studies, and also some special meetings. The starting cycle was ideal to bring the meetings into being, as the format did not require much involved preparation. Following that breathing space, the meetings programme may now need a little fine–tuning. We would suggest the following revised cycle:

- Week One: Bible study series —part 1.
- Week Two: time of prayer.
- Week Three: Bible study series —part 2.
- Week Four: special meeting.
- Week Five (if any): time of prayer.

With this new cycle, more preparation and planning is involved, and we suggest that two or three of you meet to plan a Bible study series, and to arrange a programme of special meetings for Week 4 for a year ahead. Those given this responsibility would obviously welcome ideas submitted by other members. They would first need to decide the length of the Bible study series, which should not be interminable.

Special meetings in Week Four could be made up of visiting speakers: local ministers, Christian professional specialists or businessmen —perhaps speaking on subjects which you have given them, to ensure a balanced and tailored programme. Do not hesitate to give your speakers subjects. Most of them will appreciate it. Christian videos are another possibility for Week Four, as are special services at Christmas, Easter and perhaps harvest thanksgiving. What about putting on a buffet lunch in connection with a video showing, or invited speaker, and invite your colleagues? Plan your menu, allocate items for the CF group members to bring, and this is not too difficult after all. Or come to an arrangement with the staff restaurant to supply a buffet.

Whatever you do, both with your meetings programme and your other activities, do not over–reach yourselves. Do not rush the CF group into being. Plan prayerfully and patiently, and act as though the CF group is going to last for thirty years —as many have. If you set too great a pace, it can lead to discouragement if ambitious plans do not succeed. By proceeding steadily you can gradually take on more.

With regard to your witness activities not connected with meetings, our advice is very clear: do not do everything, but do DO something. Perhaps you could start off by taking to heart one idea. For instance, you could think about some of the following:

- Send 'Get Well' cards to colleagues who are off sick or in hospital.
- Set up an intranet website, with permission of course.
- Arrange a carol, Easter or harvest service.
- Distribute Christmas cards to all employees.
- Arrange an evangelistic lunchtime seminar.
- Organise a series of 'Just Looking' events.
- Order a bulk supply of the 'Jesus Video' to give away free.

Whatever you plan, do remember to share out around all the CF group members the work involved in all the projects you take on. In that way, nothing will become a burden or chore to any one person, and everyone will feel involved.

UNDER WAY

Having read all this, maybe now is the time to call a meeting to decide what you are going to do, and to plan your timetable and consider who does what. If anyone is unable to attend, make sure you give them a full report on what was decided, as soon as practicable afterwards. This will keep them informed and involved. Also, keep looking out for previously undiscovered Christians —and keep in touch with *Christians at Work.* If you get things up and going, you might want to think about affiliation!

2

PLANNING A GROUP PROGRAMME

We now look at the development of your Christian fellowship (CF) group and assume that everything is operational and meeting regularly, whether only for the past few months or for the last twenty five years!

A group's programme normally consists of its regular meetings, but it also includes the 'out–of–meeting' activities such as those which we have mentioned previously, and which might include running a lunchtime bookstall in the foyer, sending Get Well cards to sick colleagues, or compiling a CF newsletter for distribution.

Later on in this book, we will give you some additional ideas for witness activities appropriate to a workplace. Here, however, we are concentrating on the regular programme of lunchtime CF group meetings at work, and we will assume that these are weekly, for half–an–hour, and that the group has separate arrangements for prayer during the week.

AIMS

The kind of programme planned should link in with the aim and purpose for which your CF group at work exists. Here are some reasons why CF groups exist in workplaces:

- To provide an opportunity for fellowship, support and encouragement among Christians working in the same company or organisation.

- To remind Christians that they belong to the Lord, in the midst of the many pressures and tensions of a working environment; to foster a spiritual concern for their non–Christian work colleagues; and to help Christians to live out their faith in the context of their work.

- To be a focal point of the Christian witness in a workplace, and to give opportunity to invite non–Christian colleagues to particular events and activities which might awaken an interest in the message of salvation.

- To provide Christian teaching and Bible study in order to help Christians think biblically about their work and the issues they face at work, so that they might live to a biblical pattern.

If you wish to combine all the aims listed above, the meetings programme needs to be carefully planned, to include some meetings suitable for believers, some particularly for non–Christians, and others which will be of general interest and have application to both.

To achieve the right balance, it is advisable to plan a programme at least three months (perhaps more) in advance.

Planning ahead will bring several distinct advantages:

a. It will enable the programme to be balanced;

b. Appropriate publicity to be prepared and actioned, ranging from a programme card or special posters, to a write–up in the company house journal;

c. It will give those leading the various meetings time to prepare thoroughly.

If you do not already have a committee, the best way to plan is to appoint two or three members of the CF group to meet together to arrange the programme, with all the other CF group members feeding in any ideas they may have.

REACHING THE OUTSIDER

Before detailed planning begins, it will be necessary to decide how frequently you are going to have meetings specifically with non–Christians in mind. Bearing in mind the long–term nature of the group's witness, the role of personal witness and the usefulness of the meetings that will be of general interest, most groups plan no more than half a dozen directly evangelistic meetings in a year, perhaps fewer.

VARIETY

Once the number of outreach meetings has been determined, the remaining meetings can be divided up between those specifically for Christians and those of general interest. When this has been done, the three kinds of meeting can then be provisionally dispersed through the thirteen dates for which you are compiling a three–month programme.

The next consideration is the content and style of each meeting. In the programme below, you will find six Bible studies, three discussions, two speakers, one video and one interview —five different styles of meeting. Variety of style can be as important as that of content, to prevent an impression of sameness or staleness.

The three–month programme prepared by our hypothetical CF may finally look something like this in outline:

May

- **May 5th** Bible study series on money: *The Problem of Wealth* (Luke 18:18–30).
- **May 12th** *Science, Yes; Bible, Yes* —A research biochemist talks about his faith and his work.
- **May 19th** Bible study series on money: *Enthusiastic Giving and Cheerful Restitution* (Luke 19:1–10).
- **May 26th** Discussion: *A Christian Response to the Stress Problem.*

June

- **June 2nd** Bible study series on money: *Right Stewardship of What is not our Own* (Luke 19:11–27).
- **June 9th** Video: *Journey into Faith* —the testimony of John Blanchard.
- **June 16th** Bible study series on money: *A Temple is not a Market* (Luke 19:45–46 and Mark 11:15–17).

- **June 23rd** Discussion: *Career, Church and Family —Priorities amid the Conflicts.*
- **June 30th** *Working Life in Peru* —Bill Smith–Jones (Project Engineer), back from his commissioning trip.

July

- **July 7th** Bible study series on money: *Giving to Caesar what is Caesar's* (Luke 20:20–26).
- **July 14th** *The Voice of Experience* —an interview with Fred Brown, retiring after forty years as a Christian in industry.
- **July 21st** Bible study series on money: *How to be Generous, though Poor* (Luke 21:1– 4 and Mark 12:41– 44).
- **July 28th** Discussion: What does 'going the extra mile' mean today?

The pace and range of the above sample programme is undoubtedly too intensive for many groups, but it should give you a flavour of what can be. The imaginary programme includes meetings of an evangelistic nature, such as that on June 9th, and some primarily for Christians, such as June 23rd. But there are several meetings of sufficient general interest to which colleagues can be invited without their feeling 'got at'.

Every meeting has a title, since this is a help to those leading them, and it also makes publicity much more effective. Such a programme will make the CF group meetings lively, punchy and worth attending, making all the preparatory work worthwhile. Even Christians can wilt if the programme is dull!

FEEDBACK

If possible, allow a few minutes at the end of each meeting, depending on its type and duration, for any questions or comments from those attending the meeting. This is ideal when there is a speaker, but there is no need for it at a discussion, since those burning to say something will have had opportunity during the meeting.

Five minutes should be ample for feedback, unless the speaker is controversial, or there are many 'visitors' at the meeting. Decide in advance which meetings require feedback time. It need not be laboured, however, and if no comments are forthcoming, the meeting could be closed.

VISITING SPEAKERS

When inviting outside speakers, or inside ones, do not hesitate to give them a subject that fits in with the balance of your programme. They exist to serve your witness, not you their speaking experience. Many speakers appreciate being given a topic.

Do not be deterred from inviting visiting speakers by the fear of small attendances. Really worthwhile speakers will always greatly value the efforts made by a handful of Christians to bring into their place of work the truth of God and the message of salvation. The better planned your meetings are, the better their likely quality, and the more people will be likely to come.

WISDOM NEEDED

Finally, it would be wise to take care with subjects that might appear in your publicity, however unintentionally, to appear to imply criticisms of minority groups which may be represented in your workforce. Subjects in this category include: other faiths, the cults, freemasonry, homosexuality and a number of other issues. Such subjects may arouse the concern of the management, without any real benefit to the CF group. It is not essential to address these kinds of subjects *before* communicating the gospel and it may be best to avoid such topics at work altogether, since to do so may create a counter–productive atmosphere of conflict, especially if your group has recently come into being, or the management is not particularly sympathetic to the CF group. To choose not to address particular issues in a particular setting is not to compromise on them; there will be other times and places when someone who responds to the word of God can receive fuller teaching in due course.

3

MAKING USE OF INFORMATION TECHNOLOGY IN THE WORKPLACE

IMPORTANT NOTICE —READ THIS FIRST!

The editor, compiler, publisher and *Christians at Work* declare that this chapter sets out what may be technically possible, NOT what is legally permissible in the UK or elsewhere. This book is being circulated in different countries, each of which has its own laws relating to the use, handling and storage of data. The onus is entirely upon YOU, the data user, to ensure that all data you may store, process, retrieve or disseminate is dealt with or handled only in accordance with the laws applicable in the relevant jurisdiction(s). Nothing in this book should be construed as giving advice as to what is legally permitted. The principles governing handling of information in Britain are set out on the following official website, which is a useful starting point for research:

www.informationcommissioner.gov.uk

That website sets out the principles of data protection in the light of the Data Protection Act 1998, which has changed many earlier rules and procedures. It also points you to various vital pieces of guidance and includes some helpful informative material, downloadable in PDF format. Ensure that you know the law as to whether you need to carry out an official notification of your data use activities, the rights of subjects to access data, the limitations on what information you may store; the necessity for consents by subjects; your duty to ensure security of data; prohibitions on sharing of information with other persons and organizations and across frontiers, and all the many other points you need to be aware of according to the Act (or its equivalent in the country in which you live).

It is vital to get this right, and there are penalties for contravening the law on data protection in most territories. To observe this law is also our Christian duty, of course.

There are many points which need to be checked before carrying out any IT activity involving information about persons. To think about only one of many possible examples, are you aware that (in the UK) the 1998 Act makes it clear that information concerning a person's 'religious beliefs or other beliefs of a similar nature' is defined as 'sensitive data', to which special rules apply? This is only one aspect of a huge subject to which we could not possibly do justice in this book and which we are not setting out to address here. Quite apart from the wide circulation of this resource, and the consequent variety of legislative frameworks in different countries, there is the point that, in the UK, statute law is continually added to by case law and decisions, and, in the course of this ongoing process, points are clarified. The best advice is, as always: take legal advice on any proposed IT use —from a suitably qualified person in the country where you live.

Introduction

If you have skipped the bold notice above: please go back and read it carefully before going any further. It really is essential!

Information technology (IT), as most of us now know, is just another technology for managing and communicating information (such as writing, use of the telephone, printing) and must always be subservient to the content: the medium is not the message! However, as with all new technologies, IT offers powerful new opportunities and new ways of doing the old things —but it also brings new dangers.

We are focusing here on the use of IT for Christian purposes, and not general IT issues, such as the ethical problems associated with such technology (nor the legal aspect, which, as we have seen, you need to check out for yourself). Moreover, we are concentrating on the 'communal' aspects of using IT, rather than on its use by individual Christians, since the greatest effect of IT today is in the area of interpersonal and mass communications. The intention of this chapter is to provide some basic pointers for groups that might be thinking of using IT, rather than giving detailed technical information.

What forms of IT are available for Christians to use at work?

1. **Individual PCs.**

2. **Networked PCs.** Through networks it is possible to gain access to shared areas for minutes of committee meetings, news items, bulletin boards, etc.

3. **Email** —which has potential for allowing communication within the company, and outside the company.

4. **Internet** (outside the company) —allows access to the world wide web, where many Christian resource sites can be found and linked to.

5. **Intranet** (within the company) —allows for the possibility of setting up an 'in–house' website for others to visit.

How can these forms of IT be used?

Once connected to a network, information can be shared pro–actively and reactively. Either we go to them, or they come to us! Both modes are useful.

Pro–active
We are reminded of the necessity of Christians being pro–active. ('Go into all the world....') Email is a prime medium of pro–active communication for us.

Reactive
('Always prepared to give a reason for your hope.') This is where a website is invaluable: completely under the author's control, and always available.

These two different methods can both be used in a number of different ways:

For publicity: telling others about special meetings, about the existence of the CF.

For information: answering enquirers' questions —on what we believe, for example.

For evangelism: presenting the facts of the gospel.

For fellowship: sharing between members of the CF.

For discussion, feedback: providing an opportunity to reply to questions from others and to discuss matters of concern to the fellowship.

For encouragement: keeping in touch isolated Christians or groups, and those who cannot get to meetings.

What general principles do we need to bear in mind?

1. If designing a website, the scope and aims of the CF should be clearly defined. The initial design stages are often a good time to re–evaluate what you are trying to achieve as a group.

2. Do not give unnecessary offence, and **make sure permission is obtained for use of company equipment, facilities, rooms, etc. —even time, on occasions.**

3. Take every opportunity to present a positive image of the CF (getting involved with charitable work, etc.) '...have a good reputation with outsiders' (see 1 Timothy 3:7). Be seen to be involved.

4. Be careful when and how time and resources are given to CF activities. It is always very easy for IT to become all–consuming.

What specific principles do we need to bear in mind?

Be careful to target the information.

- Draw up specific mailing lists.
- Discreetly distinguish between those who are clearly committed to the CF, those who appear to be nominal and those who are inquirers or curious. You will most likely want to send different messages to these different categories at different times!
- Make sure CF specific information does not get sent to those who will be upset or offended.
- Remember that emails can easily be forwarded, and electronic information duplicated.
- Remember that company sensitive information is best not put in electronic form.
- Use confidentiality and encryption where necessary.

Filter the information.

Not everything from outside or inside the company is suitable to repeat. Keep close editorial control of the website and email mailing lists.

For the CF website, draw up a policy and stick to it.

- Keep the site up to date: do not let it go stale. It must not be static.

- Make it visually interesting; not too much on a page; graphics slow down loading.

- Have an editorial policy, and, if possible, an editorial committee.

- Take note of the company security policy, both for those accessing information outside the company, and those outside accessing information within.

- Remember that there is an open marketplace: the 'opposition' may set out their stall and state their views, too, on the company's intranet or website.

- Do not forget those who do not have access to IT.

What are the benefits of using IT in the workplace?

1. Anonymity. People can read and browse without anyone watching or knowing (with the possible exception of company security!)

2. The ability to keep people informed even when they cannot attend meetings.

3. Up to date information can be made readily available centrally. (Posters and other printed materials are out of date as soon as the event has happened.)

4. 'Virtual' meetings can take place, whereby issues are dealt with efficiently and time is saved.

5. Evangelism opportunities open up through website pages and email invitations to outreach events.

6. You can keep in touch with those in isolated situations at the press of a button.

7. IT can enhance togetherness in a small fellowship, and help to manage a large one.

8. You never know who is 'out there'! '...some people have entertained angels without knowing it.' (See Hebrews 13:2).

What are the dangers of using IT in the workplace?

1. You really do not know who is 'out there'! As well as 'entertaining angels' you may also be giving fuel for those who would seek to accuse you. (See 1 Peter 2:12.)

2. Mailing lists do not necessarily represent the Christian Fellowship, only those who have expressed an interest in the information. Therefore, you may get a false sense of the health of the commitment of the Christian presence in your place of work.

3. IT can be made a substitute for meeting and conversation; many modern 'means of communication' can end up making people more isolated.

4. Don't let the technology obscure the message.

Finally —some ideas and suggestions

1. Think about asking a Christian who is not necessarily a regular attender of the group to take responsibility for designing a website. Giving him or her a specific responsibility might increase their commitment.

2. If you want to contact other groups who are successfully using IT, then get in touch with the *Christians at Work* office for contact details.

3. If employees have access to the internet, think about having links to some of the 'Christian apologetics' websites. (Constantly changing web addresses, but easily found using any major search engine.)

4. Why not have a FAQ page on your website with answers to 'frequently asked questions' about the Christian faith, such as:

If there is a God, why is there so much suffering?

How do I know that Christianity is right when there are so many other religions?

Isn't Christianity out of date and old–fashioned?

For concise answers to some of these types of questions, have a look at some Christian websites and links.

5. Think about distributing devotional material by email to those on your email mailing list. For a list of organisations that produce email daily devotions, or make daily devotions available online, a useful site is: **www.cybergrace.com**.

6. Have a look at some of the sites designed to help Christians use the internet, such as: **www.gospelcom.net** and explore useful links from there.

7. If you find something is working well, please let the *Christians at Work* office know, so that we can share this with other groups.

4

ORGANISING A SPECIAL SERVICE

In this chapter we are going to focus especially on the sort of services (such as carol services) that are welcome in some workplaces around the Christmas period, but many of the same considerations apply for other meetings which include worship, whether large or small, structured or informal, short or long, at lunchtime or in the evening. So in what follows, where the example of a 'carol service' is mentioned, do think about other opportunities to use appropriate forms of worship to bring the good news of our Lord Jesus Christ into the workplace. The biblical message associated with Christmas is simply one of the best examples of this kind of opportunity to bear witness.

AIM

The aim of special services, such as those which can be held for Christmas, Easter or harvest, is ultimately to present the good news of our Lord Jesus Christ —that through faith and trust in him there is salvation from sin.

Christmas carol services take advantage of the fact that during the three weeks leading up to Christmas, people's minds are full of Christmas plans: buying, baking and many other preparations. In the back of their minds, many of them still know that Christmas is about Jesus Christ, but have not given any thought to that aspect. The workplace or office carol service is an opportunity for them to do so.

It is important to have this aim clearly in mind. A special service does not exist merely to enable Christians to do something 'churchy' in the workplace. Nor is its function to give a religious flavour to the goodwill that abounds in the days prior to the Christmas or Easter break.

The good news of our Lord Jesus Christ is a clear and vital message, and should be presented firmly, focussing the attention of those present on the real meaning of Christmas—the coming of our Lord Jesus Christ into the world to save sinners. Similarly at Easter, the focus has to be on the death and resurrection of our Lord.

TIME AND PLACE

If the carol service has become a company event, it will probably take place in the evening and be attended by the management. If it is solely a CF group activity, it will be more likely to be at lunchtime or immediately after work ends for the day. In the evening it may occupy up to ninety minutes, but at lunchtime maybe only half an hour. The shorter it is at lunchtime, the more likely that people will come.

If there are split lunch breaks on your site, consider holding two carol services at different times. Depending on where people are likely to come from, different locations for the two services may also be an advantage. A venue as near as possible to the hub of activity on site is preferable. The nearer the venue, the more people are likely to come.

If this is to be your first special service, and you have no idea how many people to expect, try to obtain a room of modest size. It will be no hindrance for people to have to stand throughout, and it is better for a room to appear over–full than half–empty.

PLANNING

At your first planning meeting, which needs to take place in mid–October for Christmas and mid–February for Easter, delegate as many of the tasks as possible to different members of the CF group. This will not only encourage a sense of fellowship in the project, but will also help to ensure that one person does not have to do everything.

Book your venue well in advance, in writing if need be. Whether the venue is on the site, or in a local church hall over the road, check the booking again before your publicity is prepared, and before it goes out. This is especially necessary if your venue is within the site. Book the room for twenty minutes before and after the actual meeting times. Organise someone to prepare the meeting room in good time so that the service does not start late. Remember also to leave the room afterwards in the state and layout in which you found it.

If possible, it is always advisable to avoid having your Christmas carol service on the same lunchtime as the staff Christmas dinner, so make sure you check with the catering manager before you fix the date. This can only be done if the date for the staff dinner is fixed well in advance. Sometimes this advance catering scheduling is not done, and you will not be able to wait until early December to fix your date. So it would not be unreasonable to request the catering manager to try to avoid a clash with your date.

Another idea you may wish to consider is whether you are able to invite people from other workplaces to your carol service. If it is possible, make sure the invitation reaches them in good time, and that you remember to arrange for their admission to your site on the day of the carol service.

CONTENT

Whether it is management–patronised, or solely a CF group activity, every special service organised by a CF group at work should include a Bible–based message on a theme related to the event.

There is wide scope for an apt and powerful presentation of the heart of the gospel, even in a message of only five minutes. Ten minutes would be ample for a message in a half–hour service, with a maximum of fifteen minutes in the longest of services.

To fail to give a clear gospel presentation to those gathered is more than a wasted opportunity. It will give a long–lasting impression to people that there is nothing they need to hear; nothing to which they have not already attained. People need to go away feeling challenged concerning the hope that is available in Christ Jesus.

In addition to the message, the special service could consist of:

■ Bible reading(s). Some groups have invited a member of senior management, or local VIP (such as the local mayor) to read a passage of Scripture. This may help in your effort to publicise the event.

■ A sketch. If you are going to do this you must ensure that it is very well done. (There is nothing worse than a sketch which falls flat.)

- For a carol service, naturally, well–known carols. See below for some guidance concerning music.

- Poems or other readings.

When you plan the programme, always be careful not to over–estimate the time you have available. Decide on the overall time allowed for the service and time each item within it carefully. Do not over–run the allocated, advertised time! Remember to think about the possibility of using some time immediately after the service. Many CF groups have found it useful to be able to invite people to stay for coffee/tea and mince pies. This will allow for some follow–up conversations and relationship building.

SPEAKER

Most CF groups find it helpful to have a visiting speaker for their service —perhaps a local pastor or clergyman who, to your knowledge, presents the gospel effectively. The speaker, who ought to be contacted well in advance, should be asked to direct the message (within the allotted time slot) to the non–Christians present in a friendly, informal style. Within that friendly informality, however, the message needs to be presented in a serious and clear way. Such an explicit briefing will be appreciated by the speaker.

MUSIC

Singing will necessitate some kind of accompaniment. This could be the social club piano, a portable electronic piano or organ, an accordion, or any other instruments owned and played by members of the CF group. In the case of larger carol services, maybe the local Salvation Army band would be willing to come and play. At very small services, pre–recorded accompaniment could be provided on a CD or cassette player.

Hymn books or carol sheets can be borrowed from churches, or the words of carols can be displayed on overheads. Ideally, though, it is best to have the words to carols or hymns printed in an attractively produced programme. The programme could also give some details of what the CF group does and include any relevant announcements and the contact details of CF group members (only by permission, of course), and copies of any readings or poems used (subject to copyright restrictions).

PUBLICITY

Making the special service known and inviting people personally are two different things, but both are important. Ways of making the service known might include:

- Posters on notice boards;
- An announcement over the callover system;
- Electronic mail;
- Distribution of invitation cards.
  (This could be combined with a Christmas or Easter card, as appropriate.)

Attractive card blanks for invitation cards can be obtained from, and overprinted by: CPO, Garcia Estate, Canterbury Road, Worthing, West Sussex BN13 1BW.

For some sample card blanks and an order form, telephone 01903 264556.

If you are thinking of producing your own publicity, the *Christians at Work* office has copies of a number of cartoons which could be incorporated into posters or invitation cards. Again, please get in touch if you would like a copy of these.

Advance publicity can also be given in your staff newspaper or house journal, provided that you contact the editor by the deadline date for the December issue. Sound the editor out in good time.

At best, however, all these means are only helps. Remember that the best way of filling up the chairs at your service is for you to invite colleagues personally, during the previous week or so.

OTHER OPPORTUNITIES FOR WITNESS

- Ask the editor of your staff newspaper whether he or she would use a 'seasonal message' from the CF in its Christmas issue. Ask in good time!

- Send Christmas or Easter cards to all colleagues, including a Bible text and details of your special service.

- Present Christian calendars to members of senior management.

- At Christmas, sing carols on the office steps or at the factory gates on one or two lunchtimes prior to the carol service. If you need any help with this, contact the *Christians at Work* office and we may send Gail to lead you!

- Have a special charity appeal for a worthy cause. CaW can advise, if you wish. A collection for a Christmas hamper distribution to local sheltered housing complexes is one idea.

5

PRIORITIES FOR CHRISTIAN FELLOWSHIP GROUPS

According to Romans 12:1–2, our thinking (i.e. the renewing of our minds) makes a difference to the way we live (i.e. offering our bodies as a living sacrifice). Therefore, before thinking about priorities in practice, it is important to look at our priorities in thinking.

PRIORITIES IN THINKING

One of the key roles of a CF group is to help and encourage individual Christians to live out their faith in the places where God has called them to be.

There are a number of key needs on the part of the individual:

■ Integrated Christian living

It is relatively easy to make a split between spiritual things and secular things. We can easily see our work as a secular activity and not think about it in terms of giving glory to

God. But it is in the whole of our lives, and with our bodies, that we are called to worship and glorify God. (See 1 Corinthians 10:31; Romans 12:1). Christians who work spend most of the waking time at work (on average 88,000 hours in a lifetime), so it is crucial to work out what it means to give glory to God in and through one's work. A CF group can help the individual to do this.

- **Seeing the workplace as a place of ministry**

Ministry simply means service and in our work we are called to serve the Lord (see Colossians 3:23; Ephesians 4:11,12). Work is therefore where ministry should take place. Ministry is not something that is simply and centrally church–related. Rather it is something which is whole life related. Ministry is not something that the church minister/pastor does. Rather, it is something that all of God's people should be doing. A CF group can help remind individuals that the workplace is a key place for ministry.

- **Witness flowing from ministry**

Witness is not just something we *do*. Rather, it concerns what we *are*. (See Matthew 5:13,14; 1 Peter 3:15.) So witness is not to be seen as simply a series of interactions, such as that which might take place, for example, during a conversation with a work colleague during the lunch break, valuable as that activity may be. Witness should flow from our ministry, which has to do with the *whole* way we live and work. Again, a CF group has the potential to remind individuals of this truth.

Workplace CF groups have a great potential to help Christians make a difference in their place of work. Here are some other points of potential to think about:

■ **Worship**

As you meet together to encourage each other, see what you are doing in the context of entering into 'the Most Holy Place' by the new and living way which has been opened up for us because of what the Lord Jesus Christ has done. (Read Hebrews 10:19–25). Even as you meet together in twos or threes, think about the fact that you are taking part in an act of worship and therefore meet in a manner worthy of praise.

■ **Real fellowship**

We were not only created for fellowship with God, we were also created for fellowship with each other. (See Genesis 2:18 and Ecclesiastes 4:9–12). Through our experience of fellowship we can find the mutual support and encouragement we need to live out our faith with integrity. Many Christians fail to do this because they are alone in the workplace. We can ease one another's burdens. (Galatians 6:2.) Treat the fellowship offered by a workplace CF seriously; it is the Lord's work and in many ways just as important as any church based ministry. Do not forsake the gathering together as some are in the habit of doing. (See Hebrews 10:25).

■ **Accountability**

Despite the fact that this might not be a popular word or concept, it is vital for Christians, especially Christians who work. (See James 5:16.) Through meeting together at work, Christians can specifically pray for each other and hold each other accountable regarding their witness at work. This rarely happens at 'church'.

■ **Group outreach**

There is one thing a CF group can do that a local church cannot do, and that is to organise outreach events in a workplace. There are great opportunities for group outreach.

It should of course be remembered that in the Gospels, rather than send his first disciples out individually to witness, Jesus taught them to work together. (See Luke 9:1–6; 10:1.)

It should be remembered that the 'small group' was Jesus' model. (See Luke 6:13). He could have picked a hundred disciples out of all those who followed him, but instead chose just twelve —just a small group!

PRIORITIES IN PRACTICE

Here are some things that a CF group will need to do if it is going to truly make a difference for Jesus in the workplace.

Begin defining your aims and objectives. If you aim at nothing, the chances are that you will hit it. Many groups flounder because of a lack of agreed aims and objectives. If you are not sure where to start, then start with the basics, which are summed up in Acts 2:42:

■ **The apostles' teaching (the Scriptures)**

In the setting of a CF group you can study the Scriptures specifically from a workplace angle. For studies that will help you do this, see *Witness at Work: Bible Studies* (available from the *Christians at Work* office).

■ **Prayer**

This is the most important aspect of our support for each other. Also, in a CF group you can specifically pray for each other's work colleagues. You can pray, too, for your company and for senior management. See chapter 12, which deals specifically with prayer.

■ **Fellowship**

If *real* fellowship is to take place in the group, then this means sharing in each other's lives, being honest about our successes and failures. Opening up to others can sometimes be a bit risky, but without this kind of personal sharing we can miss out on so much blessing.

- **Breaking bread**

This can be interpreted as sharing communion, but it can also be interpreted as eating together. Arranging and sharing social activities plays an important role in bringing people together.

Note: Later on in Acts chapter 2 we read that that the disciples met together in the temple courts. This would have been a clear, visible witness to all those present in the temple at the time. Again, we see an element of group witness. (See Acts 2:46.)

One possibility for groups is a 'group covenant'. This is an agreement between members of the group regarding:

- Agreed parameters such as confidentiality, honesty, etc.,
- Agreed responsibilities such as prayer, caring, commitment, etc.,
- Agreed focus.

Leadership

Leadership is a crucial factor in the wellbeing of any group. It is amazing the difference that one committed individual can make. However, many individuals, especially those with pressure–filled jobs, want to avoid leadership to avoid responsibilities. But leadership does not necessarily mean more responsibility. Remember, the first principle of biblical leadership is plurality and delegation! Perhaps there may be one leader, but supported by one or two others.

Leadership can be undertaken by a small group of individuals, but whatever form it comes in, there must be positive leadership!

Intentional unity

It is vitally important to focus on what you have in common. We are united by the one who is himself the truth, through the Spirit. Avoid areas of contention and denominational difference at work, but do be clear about the essentials of the gospel! It might be a good idea to adopt a Basis of Faith, such as the one used by *Christians at Work*. Also, think about activities that would encourage unity.

Have an outward focus

It is easy for a smaller group to get into a rut by becoming too inward looking. It has been said that, 'The church exists by mission as a flame exists by burning.' This is also surely true of a workplace CF group.

Be prepared to use your imagination and be prepared to take risks! It is astonishing how much difference an outward focus can make in terms of purpose and unity. Here are just a few ideas for outreach. You may think of many others.

■ Buffet lunch with invited speaker

■ Lunchtime or evening seminar

■ Christianity Explained/Explored type courses

- Christmas events
- Easter events
- Harvest thanksgiving events
- Exhibition stands at open or family days
- A give–away book or video table
- Outreach sports outings
- Intranet website

Focus on relationships

a. Group members

Remember that when God brings us into relationship with himself, he also calls us into relationship with each other! Always remember that people are more important than programmes. Love is the priority in the life of the Christian (see John 13:35), and showing self–sacrificial love should be a priority for leaders and members of a CF group.

b. Non–Christian work colleagues

Being relationship focused is crucial to our witness. Jesus always had time for people. He did not come and organise a programme. Rather, he came and he spent time with people. Remember that God did not save us in some impersonal way. Rather, the Father sent his own Son. Jesus came and lived among us. (Re–read John 1:1–15).

Supporting one another

Oftentimes, the pressure of work, home and church can lead even the finest and most balanced of Christian men or women to the point of sheer desperation and depression. Sharing these feelings is never easy. Depression is so often viewed by the world as a sign of weakness, and all too often by Christian people it is viewed critically and judgmentally as a sign of some unconfessed sin, when in reality it is most often the sign of being overwhelmed and overworked by the extreme pressures of life —and being a Christian does not exempt us from such conditions. As a people, we know that if we are in regular communication with God then these things can be somewhat easier for us to deal with, but being overwhelmed by the pressures of this world can bring a very personal sense of breakdown in relationship with God, and this is where we need help —not least to regain an awareness of the constancy of his love.

It should be a priority to pray for one another, and if an atmosphere of trust has been built up within the groups then it should be possible to bear one another's burdens by sharing our worries and concerns and praying for each other. Of course this has to be done in an atmosphere of genuine humility, trust and love.

6

A BIBLE STUDY IN TWENTY MINUTES

"A Bible study? But we've only got twenty minutes...." Most meetings of most Christian Fellowship groups in workplaces take the form of discussion–based Bible studies. However, pressures on time have led many to feel that the life is being squeezed out of the Bible study.

Does that have to be the case? Can you have a Bible study in just twenty minutes? The answer to the latter question must be 'Yes', but there are important matters that need to be carefully thought through and wisely implemented.

Here are some questions and points to consider:

Who is the study for, and what are its aims?

Without a clear focus, the meeting will drift along without really helping anyone. You can aim to cater for Christians, enquirers or both. This needs to be one of the first decisions made in planning a Bible study. You may want to vary the emphasis of the meetings, but it is wiser to concentrate on one group in each series of studies.

Having decided for whom the study is going to be, you need to decide what the study is meant to achieve. Clearly you will want believers to be built up and unbelievers to be converted.

But these aims need to be fleshed out a little more. Consideration needs to be given to where those attending are in their own Christian life. Are they mature believers or relatively new Christians? If you are meeting with unbelievers, what is their background in relation to Christian things? These questions need to be answered before you decide how and what to study.

What is the most effective format?

With only twenty minutes, it is impossible to have a mini–service, however desirable you may feel that to be. But you must pray and seek the Lord's blessing on your fellowship and study. If time is not going to defeat you, you also need to concentrate on the passage you are studying. It may be that the leader will begin by speaking for two or three minutes to introduce the topic or passage, or perhaps to recap on the previous study. The rest of the time can then be spent in fruitful discussion, concluding with prayer.

Using that 'introduction/discussion' format, each member of the group will feel free to contribute to the discussion as they are able, but there must be clear, effective leadership. Alternatively, the group might find it helpful to consider using most of the allotted time to receive Bible teaching from someone with a clear gift of teaching. This might be followed by one or two questions to the speaker and then a short time of prayer/ministry. If we term this the 'speaker format' then it could be used not only when visiting speakers come but also by in–house group members. It will become clear which members really do have a gifting for this; no–one should be pressured into teaching who does not feel a call to it; but if the group does have some who are mature and clearly very effective in the role, they can sometimes be asked to teach in that more extended way (but still within the overall twenty minute period). Of course, great sensitivity and discretion is needed on the part of the people doing the planning and inviting, however often or rarely this format is used.

What passages should we study?

With the Scriptures, it really is a case of 'spoilt for choice'. However, certain portions will be more suited to the group's situation. Choose your material in a thoughtful way, paying due regard to your aims and those likely to be present.

There are three main types of Bible study that you could adopt: consecutive, topical or character studies.

a. Consecutive Study

A book or passage is selected and studied systematically over a period of time. Be careful how you handle longer books; you may want to split them into shorter sections and study each section on its own, perhaps with other material in between. Here are some suggestions for consecutive study:

Old Testament:

- Some of the shorter books can be studied right through—for example Ruth, Ezra, Ecclesiastes, Jonah, and Haggai. In the longer books, you may find it helpful to study smaller portions such as Genesis 1–11; Exodus 1–15; I Samuel 1–7.

- With the Psalms, there is a great variety and a number of series can be planned.
- The longer prophets need care, and it may help to study them thematically through selected portions.

New Testament:

- In the Gospels, try series such as *People Jesus Met; The Incarnation; The Death and Resurrection of Jesus; Parables; Miracles; The I am' Sayings; Sermon on the Mount; In the Upper Room.*
- With the book of Acts, there are clearly defined sections that can be studied as a series (see any good commentary).
- In the Epistles, try some of the shorter ones to begin with, such as Philippians, Colossians, I Thessalonians, James, I Peter, I John. Make sure you keep the flow of the argument in mind, and try not to get bogged down. You may choose to study just one part of a letter.
- With Revelation, a series on the seven letters (chapters two and three) would be very useful.

b. Topical Study

There are many approaches you could take.

- You could aim to be directly evangelistic and look at topics such as *Who was Jesus?* or *How do I get to Heaven?*

- Or you could take current issues from an evangelistic perspective, such as *Is there Hope for the Family?* or, *Why Does God Allow Suffering?*

- For Christians, practical issues such as *The Christian and Work, Witnessing; Walking Worthily*, or *Biblical Praying*, can be very stimulating and beneficial.

It would also be possible to do a series of studies in basic Christian doctrine, perhaps along the lines of Bruce Milne's *Know the Truth* (IVP), which could then be used as a study guide.

c. Character Studies

This is a very useful way of studying material in some of the longer books without covering the whole book. Subjects abound in the pages of Scripture —Abraham, Jacob, Joseph, Moses, Joshua, David, Elijah, Elisha, Mary, Paul, Peter, etc. Why not tackle some of the lesser-known figures, too?

Who can best lead the Bible Study, and how?

Leadership is very important. The leader must be a spiritual person, well versed in the Scriptures and capable of handling the discussion format (if that is the format to be employed). Ideally, they will have some experience of leading such a group in their own church and have the support of the leaders of that church.

Should a keen young Christian with potential be allowed to lead? Again, this needs careful consideration. It can be a useful way of gaining experience and serving the Lord, but needs to be handled wisely. If you elect to give an enthusiastic beginner a chance, there should be another leader present who is able to step in and give help when needed and to offer constructive criticism privately, in an acceptable way, in the course of time.

The leader really does need to lead, not simply to chair a discussion. So many small group Bible studies fail at this point. 'Leading' does not mean dominating the discussion (although the leader may say more than other folk) but involves guiding the discussion in a purposeful way, responding helpfully to other people's contributions and explaining any points of difficulty in the text. The leader must always be sensitive to the needs of those present.

Keeping to time and using it well.

The real problem here is not keeping to time in absolute terms. All you need for that is a little group discipline and a good alarm clock! However, it is vital that the time is well used and that, as far as possible, you cover the intended ground.

Beware of digressions. Some can be helpful, but not all. Try to stick to the subject in hand; a well–chosen passage or theme will provide enough suitable material for discussion. Good leadership is essential here, but so too is the self–discipline of each group member. Always look for the main point in the passage.

In the introduction/discussion format, it will be vital for each member of the group to prepare in advance, not just the person doing the introduction. Without this, the study may be nothing more than a case of pooled ignorance! Notes and questions on the passage being distributed in advance can help this. You may want the group to use a ready made study guide (see Resources below), or you may want the leader(s) to put some notes and questions together.

Resources

There are many Bible study booklets and notes available, e.g. the Lifebuilder series. Some popular commentaries now have a study section included at the end. (Many volumes in *The Bible Speaks Today* series now include this). A number of volumes in the Welwyn Commentary series are ideal for the leader to use, and contain suggestions.

Did you know that there are several Bible study outlines produced by *Christians at Work*, covering many relevant topics? There are three series, each with seven studies, especially designed for lunchtime workplace groups:

Series 1: Studies in the Old Testament

Series 2: Studies in the New Testament

Series 3: Studies in the Life of Joseph

Again, from the *Christians at Work* office, you can order a copy of *Witness and Work Bible Studies.*

Visit your local Christian bookshop and examine what is available. But remember your aims, and be discerning.

7

IDEAS FOR WORKPLACE WITNESS AND OUTREACH

Here we list just some of the basic and relatively simple ideas for workplace witness and outreach:

BADGES

Wearing a fish badge has a well proven track record for provoking conversation; or, indeed, the badge of a recognised Christian organisation will help to identify you to other Christians in workplaces that are too large to allow you to know everyone personally. Badges can also provoke inquiries from, and conversation with, non–Christians. Why not put a *Christians at Work* logo on your car windscreen! Somebody even put one on their office door —a bright coloured fish with the words '@ work' in the centre. Such signs are inoffensive and yet, to Christians, meaningful — and another conversation starter!

BUILDING UP FRIENDSHIPS

Building up a friendship is the most important starter for effective witness. There are many ways in which this can be done. One would be to invite a colleague to have a meal with you at your home. Another way is to arrange a game of golf or some other sport. On the basis of friendship, colleagues so invited may be willing to attend a service at your church or a CF group event. It is a well attested fact that at least 70% of people who have come to know the Lord Jesus Christ as their Saviour had been befriended by a Christian.

TAPES

Why not pass on a good quality tape containing the testimony or helpful comments of a 'high profile' Christian? LICC produce a series of tapes entitled 'Making Waves'. Among those who talk about their faith are Fiona Castle, Hans Sagers (goalkeeper for Wimbledon, Wolves and Spurs), Tom Kelly and James Tate. For more details contact the *Christians at Work* office.

CHRISTIANITY EXPLAINED/EXPLORED COURSES

A number of groups have run a variety of 'Introduction to Christianity' courses —and have seen their non–Christian work colleagues come along! These courses can be run during lunchtime or after work. One group put on a light buffet meal after work and followed this up with the course. The *Christians at Work* office has details of several introductory courses, including: Christianity Explained; Christianity Explored; Just Looking; Simply Christianity, and Staying Alive. The *Alpha* course might also be considered.

BIBLES AND CHRISTIAN BOOKS

Bibles or good Christian books can be presented as gifts to colleagues getting married, retiring, or leaving the company, or to VIP visitors. Some companies allow Bibles to be placed permanently in medical rooms or reception areas.

CD–ROMS

Rather than a book or tape, why not give the person with whom you work an evangelistic CD–ROM. One example is '2 Ways to Live —The Choice we all Face', a multimedia CD–ROM produced by the Good Book Company and aimed at helping people understand the central message of the Christian faith. It includes testimony videos and answers to popular questions. For more details contact The Good Book Company (020 8942 0880) or email: info@thegoodbook.co.uk. This product is available at just £5 plus postage and packing when you mention *Christians at Work*.

STRESS EVENING

SALT (the Stress and Life Trust) is a Christian organisation that runs courses and seminars on the subject of stress. 'Living Successfully with Pressure, Change and Stress' is one of their evening presentations. It is a fast moving, punchy presentation of practical and effective strategies for handling life's fast pace and pressures. It leads on naturally to finish with a short gospel message. This could be organised for the workplace or a nearby local church. Contact details for SALT will be found on p. 127.

THE 'JESUS' VIDEO

The Jesus film or video, based on the Gospel of Luke, has now been seen by an estimated 1.6 billion people. The Jesus video can now be ordered at a subsidised price of £1 per copy to groups or churches that are willing to distribute it. A special introduction and ending has been added to highlight the relevance of the Lord Jesus Christ to today's society. A Christian Fellowship group left free copies on a table in the foyer of their workplace and had over fifty names to follow up. To order, see contact details at the end of Chapter eight.

An alternative to distributing the video would be to show parts of it during the lunch break over, say, a four–week period, with time for questions and, if appropriate, ministry, afterwards.

OTHER VIDEOS

Suitable videos short enough to be shown in a lunch break at work are not plentiful. Careful research is required. We deal in detail with this in Chapter 8, which, as well as giving guidelines, also gives details of sources. Always see a video yourself before showing it, to check content and technical quality. Do not assume that every video from a Christian producer is necessarily reliable.

BOOKS AND BOOKSTALL

Giving or lending thoughtfully selected Christian books may be a way of introducing colleagues to an understanding of the gospel. An occasional bookstall may be permitted by management in a canteen, corridor or foyer, giving opportunity for a CF group to give, lend or sell books, and to talk with those who browse.

BUFFET LUNCH/SUPPER

This requires flair and forward planning. Printed personal invitations could be issued to named colleagues, inviting them to a supper one evening arranged by a group of Christians. The programme could include a talk by a member of the senior management who is a Christian. This kind of event has many benefits, not least that of welding the CF group together in a common purpose over the necessarily long period of detailed preparation.

CALENDARS

Many kinds of Christian calendar exist, and these can be placed on desks, walls, machines, and possibly in other places, where the Bible verses may be a 'silent witness' to anyone who pauses to read them. The great thing about calendars is that employees do not usually require permission to place calendars on their own desks or machines. An excellent Proverbs calendar is available as a screensaver (free of charge) from The Jubilee Centre at www.jubilee-centre.org.

SPECIAL SERVICES

This topic has been dealt with in an earlier chapter, but we underline here the point that many people are willing at Christmas, Easter or harvest time to hear something about the Lord Jesus Christ. Carol services can be varied in content and style to suit circumstances. They can be held in staff restaurants while the audience is eating lunch, or in a separate room or nearby church to which colleagues can be invited. *Christians at Work* can supply a useful pack of poems, cartoons, sketches and sample orders of service.

TEARCRAFT, FAIRTRADE OR MISSION STALL

A number of CF groups have found it valuable to organise a stall for Tearcraft (or another Christian–based organisation) or a mission stall. This kind of stall is often best located at the entrance to the canteen. Such a stall will help CF group members make contact with the rest of workforce and will be a witness to the fact that Christians care about issues relating to the developing world. Easter time is a good period for running such a stall, and this can be combined with the promotion of an Easter outreach event. You can contact Tearcraft on 0845 3558355; email: enquiry@tearfund.org.

COMPANY EVENTS

Many companies have an Open Day, gala day or similar annual event on a Saturday in the summer or autumn. CF groups are usually allowed a display stand at such events. From these stands, it may be possible to provide refreshments, show videos, arrange Bible competitions for children, or simply chat to some of the thousands of visitors at the event and give literature to contacts made. This issue is dealt with in detail in Chapter 9.

GREETINGS CARDS

Many kinds of cards exist: get well cards, Christmas cards, Easter cards, sympathy cards, retirement cards, and several others. Sent by individual Christians or by a CF group, these are almost always appreciated by the colleagues who receive them, and forge a strong link between the sender(s) and the recipient. Christmas cards could be sent, appropriately worded, to the whole workforce, if your funds permit this.

HOSPITAL AND SICK VISITING

In large workplaces there is always likely to be at least one member of staff away from work, in hospital, or at home on sick leave. A visit at such times is often welcomed, even if the employee concerned is not an immediate colleague of the Christian who visits him. Illness often proves to be a point in people's experience when they are seeking God, and the Christian visitor may find an opportunity for a caring and spiritual ministry. Although this is a time–consuming activity, it is an immensely worthwhile ministry.

LITERATURE/NEWSLETTER DISTRIBUTION

Most Christians have been involved at one time or another in the distribution of Christian literature. Choosing a book or booklet to pass on to individual contacts at work is one approach. Another is giving out tracts. A third is to produce your own leaflet to give to colleagues. A CF group could have a regular newsletter, incorporating helpful ministry articles, testimonies, programme details, names and extension numbers of CF group contacts (with permission), and any other relevant information. Whatever the reaction, this would at least ensure that everyone knew that the CF group existed, and what it represented.

WEBSITE

A number of CF groups now have their own intranet website. As well as letting the rest of the workforce know about your activities, a website can be used in a specifically evangelistic way —for example, by answering FAQs about Christianity or by pointing enquirers to books specially written for non–Christians.

NEWSPAPER AND HOUSE JOURNAL ARTICLES

House journal editors are often happy to receive submitted material. A write–up about the CF group's history, purpose or present activities would be likely to be published, and future meetings could also be 'trailed'.

8

USING CHRISTIAN VIDEOS/ DVDs IN THE WORKPLACE

Throughout this chapter, for 'video' please substitute 'DVD' where appropriate.

Why Show a Video?

Possible purposes can include:

- Evangelism
- Communicating the message of the Bible
- Showing care and concern for people
- Giving an added awareness of the CF group's presence in the workplace
- Stirring up uncommitted Christians
- Teaching and encouraging the CF group.

Technical basics: facilities and equipment

- Use a big enough screen. The screen diagonal measurement should be between one–fifth and one–tenth of the distance to the furthest viewer.

- Place the screen at a reasonable height, as it is frustrating not to be able to see past the head of the person in front.

- If you have the use of a large room with a projection video, it will take much longer to set up, and expert help may be needed.

- Always check the sound for volume beforehand, and if possible the tone, remembering that some present may have hearing defects.

- Ideally, place lighting behind or on a level with the monitor television, so that people see the screen silhouetted, which gives a clear, eye–catching picture.

- The room itself should not be so dark as to prevent people from finding their seats without tripping over, or to make it a struggle to find the exit in an emergency.

- If using a remote control, make sure you are sufficiently familiar with the buttons to be able to adjust both the sound and picture in half light! Incompetent handling of the equipment distracts the people and hinders the message.

- Check the technical quality of the tape on a reliable machine as soon as you receive it, by fast–forwarding the tape to the very end, and then rewinding back to the beginning before watching it. A tape that may not have been played for a while can become sticky and needs to be loosened up.

- You also need to know what is on the tape, as a labelling fiasco could be embarrassing.

- Check that everything works, in good time before the presentation is due to start, especially if leads have to be removed and inserted.

- Before presentation, play the tape to where you want it to start, and also be aware of where to stop the tape.

- Be prepared to have another kind of meeting if the room suddenly becomes unavailable, or you cannot make the equipment work.

Some people may come to a video rather than to a Bible study. Groups should know why they are showing a particular video, and for whom it is intended, and should plan thoroughly how the individuals—or target group—are to be invited.

Planning for Effective Use

- As suggested above, always watch the video beforehand to consider its suitability and soundness of content, rather than relying solely on promotional notes and recommendations.

- Be careful of videos which have become dated, and therefore lose their impact.

- Videos should not be used to make people feel trapped.
- A ten minute video could be used as a discussion starter, or to elicit questions.
- Science–based videos that emphasise creation are useful, especially in workplaces with a scientific context, and with people who are used to thinking issues through.
- Difficulties in obtaining videos of sufficiently short duration may sometimes be overcome by splitting longer videos into two parts.
- A cautionary note: avoid videos that address issues that are not specifically or necessarily relevant to your workplace —e.g. freemasonry, homosexuality, other religions. Whilst your Christian view of these issues is important, to present material that is overtly critical, especially on company premises, will more than likely transgress your company's operational policies on these issues, and could lead to disciplinary action if taken to the extreme. An unwise choice of subject could appear as antagonistic to a minority group. This is nothing to do with compromising biblical or personal views, but has much to do with the UK law, and could cause problems with the management, for no benefit to the CF group.

Video selection

- Many Christian bookshops and resource centres have lists of videos that are available for hire. These lists give the duration, subject matter and, when appropriate, target age group.
- Nowadays a number of churches have video libraries, and some even video their own meetings, the sermon element of which may be suitable for showing in the workplace.
- In choosing a video, have in mind what is relevant to the people working on your site. The closer the link with the work they are involved in, and the actual circumstances of their lives, the better.

Videos can be divided into three basic categories: evangelistic; contemporary and topical issues; teaching.

a. Evangelistic

There are a number of videos available from the Christian Television Association, in which well–known Christians give their testimonies. See contact details at the end of this chapter.

b. Contemporary and Topical Issues

Care for the Family has a number of video series dealing with contemporary issues, which can be used evangelistically or for teaching purposes. For example, *Beating Burnout* is a set of three videos featuring Rob Parsons, which deals with the issue of stress. See contact details at the end of this chapter.

c. Teaching

If you are looking for a teaching course on evangelism then check out John Blanchard's *School of Personal Evangelism* video series. These five videos last forty five minutes and are available from Christian Ministries. Also aiming to encourage believers to share their faith is a series of short talks by Ian Knox of the 40:3 Trust, under the title *Go For It.*

One teaching video which has been very much appreciated by workplace groups has been *God@Work*. Another, more recent, production is *Christian Life & Work*, produced by Mark Greene and available from London Bible College.

There are also videos available of well known Christian teachers such as Charles Swindoll, John MacArthur, Tony Campolo and Ulf Ekman.

Publicity

It is useful to publicise videos through suitable posters, and by personal invitation. An interesting title or subject is essential for outreach. Publicity in workplaces should state the length of the video presentation, so that people know the overall time commitment if they attend. The publicised timing should be strictly adhered to, otherwise people may feel that the CF group has taken advantage of them over timings, and they may not come again.

Follow–up

If it is not possible to have questions (or, if appropriate, discussion) at the end of the video showing, the next meeting can be devoted to this. Preparing a handout highlighting the key points will help to refresh memories, and avoid going off at tangents.

USEFUL CONTACT DETAILS

Agapé Community Initiative
incorporating the **Jesus Video Project**
Fairgate House, Tyseley, Birmingham B11 2AA
Tel. 0121 765 4404
Email: jvp@agape.org.uk www.agape.org.uk

L'Abri Cassettes (Francis Schaeffer and others)
The Manor House, Greatham, Liss GU33 6HF
Tel. 01420 538436

Grace to You, Europe
2 Caxton House, Wellesley Road, Ashford TN24 8ET
Tel. 01233 662262
Email: info@gty.org.uk www.gty.org.uk
(Re: John MacArthur)

God@Work, and Christian Life & Work
London Bible College
Green Lane, Northwood, Middlesex HA6 2UW
Tel. 01923 456000
Email: enquiries@londonbiblecollege.ac.uk
www.londonbiblecollege.ac.uk

Care For the Family
PO Box 488 Cardiff CF15 7YY
Tel. 029 2081 0800
Email: mail@cff.org.uk www.care-for-the-family.org.uk

Christian Television Association
Wraxall, Bristol BS48 1PG
Tel. 01275 851222
Email: info@cta.uk.com www.cta.uk.com
(operate a free loan library)

9

THE COMPANY OPEN DAY

WHAT IS AN OPEN DAY?

There are many types of company, but it seems there is only one type of Open Day—a combination of putting the company's own activities on show, and the provision of a variety of entertainments and activities specially imported for the occasion, to be enjoyed.

WHO WILL BE PRESENT?

Some Open Days are open to the general public, and some only to employees, their families and accompanied guests. If the event is limited to employees and families, the Christians on the stand may already know a larger proportion of their visitors.

PLANNING

Start planning for your Open Day stand at least three months before the event. The best way to plan is to get several people together to pray over and discuss ideas and arrangements.

Talk to the Open Day organisers or management as early as possible in the planning stages. You may find that they are eager to help you, and will provide all the facilities you need.

When the event arrives, make sure you set up the stand in good time —either the night before or early on the day itself. Problems can easily be resolved, as long as you do not discover them at the last minute!

WHAT DO YOU NEED?

1. A location for your stand

A strategic location, on a main thoroughfare or near to major attractions, is particularly helpful, as it will ensure you have a steady stream of passers–by all day.

2. A display

Something eye–catching, of good quality, and relevant to your workplace, but also conveying something of the essence of what your CF Group is about. A map showing where there are CF groups on other sites within the same company around the country, or in different companies locally, would arouse some interest.

A display depicting the history of the CF Group within the company, especially if the CF group was celebrating a landmark, such as a 25th anniversary, is another possibility.

3. People to man the stand

Most groups find that a rota system throughout the day, with a few manning the stand for one or two hours at a time, works best. Encourage all the Christians in your workplace to be involved in some way. Prepare a briefing sheet to give to all those involved, explaining everything they need to know.

4. Literature

Do not have too many different give–away items. Keeping it simple has proved to be most effective. One main give–away item, together with good quality back–up tracts and booklets, (available from your local Christian bookshop), have proved sufficient in practice, along with special items for children. Make sure everyone knows what literature is being used, and ensure that no–one brings their own private supply of other items. Give the team an opportunity to see the literature in advance, so that they are familiar with it.

WHAT IS THE CF GROUP STAND DESIGNED TO ACHIEVE?

There are several aims that a Christian Fellowship could have in mind in the course of their planning:

- Making the most of the opportunity for direct evangelism in informal conversation with visitors to the stand. The emphasis needs to be on the *informal* since anything inappropriately confrontational will be out of keeping with the character of the Open Day event, where the atmosphere is relaxed and friendly.

- Publicising the fact that the Christian Fellowship exists, and a little of its purpose and activities.

- Indirect evangelism, by the distribution of tracts or copies of *Challenge* newspaper, or something similar.

- Selling Christian books and other items, either as an even more indirect means of evangelism, an eye-catching attraction to the stand, or just for its own sake.

HOW ARE THE AIMS TO BE ACHIEVED?

All these aims are valid, but if you adopt more than one, pursue each of them separately, since they can conflict. For instance, if you aim to have informal spiritual conversations with visitors, make positive arrangements to help this to happen. Experience has shown that few spiritual conversations arise naturally from giving out copies of newspapers or from selling books. This need not be a problem, since opportunities for conversation will occur if you plan for them.

a. Planning for informal conversations

Depending on how much space you have available, create a seating area with a few comfortable chairs. These could be arranged informally, but so that they can easily be moved to allow, say, two 'one–to–one' conversations at a time. If a group of people arrives, the chairs can always be re–arranged. Provide free hot or cold drinks. This will give you a reason for inviting someone to sit down.

Why should anyone be willing to sit down and chat? There

are several possible reasons: walking around a large industrial site is extremely tiring; a cup of coffee is always alluring; and people who have not met for several years may well want to exchange news of each other.

At a company Open Day, it will not be surprising if every CF group member on the stand sees 15–20 people with whom they are acquainted during the day, but whom they had not seen for some while. Some of these may want to stop for a longer chat. How can such conversations turn to spiritual things? Conversations in the circumstances outlined above may cover many areas of life, and possibly a fairly long time-span. This can lead to opportunities to ask the person a question that will bring the whole conversation onto a spiritual plane. If, for instance, they have been telling you about major decisions in life that they have found difficult, ask them if they have ever thought about praying about them. If they have told you about a daughter going to university, tell them there is a CU there, and ask how they would feel if she came back a Christian? There are many more circumstances that would lead to the opportunity for spiritual conversation. If such opportunities come, apply the gospel personally and clearly, though sympathetically, to your visitor.

b. Planning for making the CF group known

This aspect is particularly important if only employees and their families attend the Open Day, since it will be more relevant to more of the people you will meet. Prepare a small leaflet, explaining where and how frequently the CF group meets, why it exists, and outlining the programme for the next few months. Keep these in an accessible place, and ask every team member to give one to each visitor who works on the site.

c. Distributing literature

The best item of literature could be a tract which you produced yourselves, relevant to the industry in which you work. Or it could be written about, or by, someone involved in your industry. Any leaflet needs to contain and convey the gospel clearly, and in an interesting and relevant way. Appropriate tracts may be available from tract distributors, and *Challenge* newspaper is particularly useful to give to readers of tabloids. You will need to consider what is most appropriate. Endeavour to give something to everyone who visits your stand, whether or not they stay for a chat.

d. Bookstalls

The danger of a bookstall is that it can dominate everything, and can prevent (a), (b) and (c) taking place. This would be sad, as it is, of the four possible aims, the least significant evangelistically. The answer to this is to have your bookstall on one side, rather than in a central position, so that the stand is seen to be not merely a bookstall. Put someone on the bookstall whose job is solely to look after that. This leaves others free to talk to people, explain displays and give out literature.

One group stopped having a bookstall after they found it confused the casual visitor to be confronted with some things free, and other things that they had to buy. Also, the casual passer–by had too little time to study a bookstall. This same group thought that a bookstall would work better where people had lots of time, and the CF group stand had plenty of space.

OTHER POSSIBILITIES

- Showing a video. One group showed the video *Journey into Life* based on the booklet by Norman Warren. This had obvious evangelistic content, was eye-catching, and could be a conversation starter as people stopped to watch for a few moments. The twelve minute Fact and Faith videos are also quite appropriate.

- Giving away balloons. This has proved to be a 'people–puller'. Some thought needs to be given to what you do with the people you attract, and whether you have anything printed on the balloons.

- Fun slides. One group installed a fun slide for children, charging 20p per child but giving as many slides as they wanted. This brought a lot of children to the stand, and some parents. Some conversations resulted. Naturally, any group planning such an activity would need to give thought to how they arranged it. A seating area for chats with the adults while the children enjoyed the slide? Check out insurance aspects in advance.

- Colouring books and bookmarks for children. These are available, with Bible themes and texts, from Christian bookshops.

- Produce a news sheet, relevant to your company, presenting a variety of useful Christian material, including details of your CF programme, and some names and contact numbers (with permission).

PRACTICAL TIPS

- If you are using a power supply, take plenty of extension leads with you.

- If the company allocates you furniture for your stand, find a way of making sure it doesn't 'walk'. A cloth would achieve this for a table.

- Last, but by no means least, try to ensure that everyone who will be taking a turn of duty manning the stall is aware of the need for the right approach. Much harm can be done if the CF group member on duty presents a dour or glum image! Members should think about the kind of attitude that they themselves would like to encounter if they were were strangers to Christian life and faith: joyful whilst not effusive; positive, whilst not inappropriately forceful; demonstrating great sensitivity to enquirers and visitors; and, above all, marked by the kind of compassion that Jesus showed to all.

10

FORTY FOUR SUGGESTIONS FOR CHRISTIAN FELLOWSHIP GROUPS IN THE WORKPLACE

Whilst some of the ideas in this chapter appear elsewhere in this book, you can use this as a checklist, or to start some discussion going, about which suggestions might usefully be employed or adapted in your own particular situation.

FINDING CHRISTIANS

1. Make a list of all the known Christians in your workplace, and their location details. Circulate a copy of that list to each of them (having obtained requisite permissions, and ensuring that you observe all data protection laws: see important cautionary note at the opening of Chapter Three).

2. Ensure that everyone on the list receives a regular copy of *net.working* (the newsletter of *Christians at Work*) every two months, either personally or through the internal mail.

3. If there are local evangelically minded churches not yet represented in your Christian Fellowship, ask the church leaders whether they have any members who work in your workplace.

4. Seek to make contact with Christians at other sites within your company or group of companies.

5. Arrange for an introductory card about the CF group to be given to all new recruits to the company with their induction pack.

PROGRAMME

6. If you do not already have a printed programme, plan a draft programme for the next three months, type it out, and circulate copies to all known Christians.

7. Photocopy this list of suggestions and circulate it to all the Christians in your group, asking them to mark up those ideas that they consider to be worth discussing or pursuing.

8. Agree as a group to read one chapter of *Thank God it's Monday* by Mark Greene each week, and have a time of feedback during your group meetings.

STRENGTHENING FELLOWSHIP

9. Arrange a social get–together for the Christians in your company, along with husbands and wives.

10. Each month, have a member of the CF group share their life story through photographs or other meaningful objects or things.

PRAYER

11. In addition to your regular CF group meetings, start a prayer time if you do not already have one, to pray for the conversion of your colleagues. Even ten minutes a week would be valuable.

12. If you are on a big site, pray with those Christians working fairly near to you.

13. Allocate the names of other staff members to members of your CF, for prayer (observing data protection/privacy rules here, as in all activities).

14. Make up a weekly prayer schedule and ask each member of the CF group to write down a prayer request for a particularly stressful part of his or her week, and agree to pray for him or her at that time.

15. Advertise the fact that the CF group is willing to receive prayer requests about any subject from any of the workforce. Work out an effective and confidential way to receive the prayer requests.

NOTICE BOARDS

16. Make sure that the notices on your notice boards are current, and that they include a contact name and internal telephone number.

17. Put a note on the bottom of your notice board posters, inviting prayer requests, with the name of the person to whom these should be given.

18. Use part of your notice board space to display a verse of Scripture or a thought–provoking poster.

19. Photocopy your CF notices onto Day–Glo paper (approx. 70p per A3 sheet from a stationer) to make them stand out.

IT

20. Appoint someone to distribute a thought for the day email available from one of the many Christian internet sites. (See *Christians at Work* group resource paper No. 3 for more details.)

21. Send out an intranet email reminder to all individuals on your CF group mailing list regarding each week's meeting.

BIBLES

22. Present your managing director with a Bible, perhaps to mark a special occasion, like your CF's Silver Jubilee, or his own appointment to the post.

23. Consider presenting a Bible to any colleague who is getting married.

CHRISTMAS

24. Start thinking now about your plans for Christmas. Consider a date and venue for a carol service or Christmas meeting.

25. Consider producing a Christmas card for distribution to your colleagues in December. This could contain a brief message, a greeting, and an invitation to your carol service, giving details.

26. Inquire whether the editor of your house journal or staff newspaper will accept a devotional article or 'seasonal message' for the Christmas issue, and arrange for someone to write it.

27. Offer to organise the official company carol service, and make sure you have freedom with regard to the programme and the speaker.

HOUSE JOURNALS

28. Announce your CF meetings in the company's house journal or staff newspaper.

29. Write a letter to your house journal or staff newspaper commenting from a Christian point of view on something you have read about in a previous issue.

30. Review a book by or about a Christian connected with your profession or your manufacturing/service sector and submit it either to your company newspaper or your professional journal.

OTHER WITNESS IDEAS

31. Plan to put some Christian calendars up in your workplace next year. These will be obtainable from Christian bookshops and by mail order. Do not leave this until December 31st! Buy them in September.

32. Buy a bulk order of evangelistic tapes —maybe the testimony of Bernard Langer (part of the Making Waves series produced by ICC) and, subject to any necessary copyright permission, make copies for distribution to colleagues.

33. Write a letter for publication in your professional or trade journal, linking an aspect of your work or expertise to a truth of God's word.

34. Consider arranging a social event to which you could invite non–Christian colleagues, just to get to know them a little better and to meet them informally.

35. Find out which of your colleagues are in hospital or on prolonged sick leave, and send a card to each one on behalf of the Christian Fellowship at work.

36. Show your genuine but not overpowering concern for those of your colleagues who appear to have particular personal problems. Remember them in prayer.

37. Find out if your company intends to have a sports day or Open Day in the coming year, and begin to plan towards how you can best present a witness for the occasion.

CHRISTIANS AT WORK

38. Make arrangements for your group to be represented at the next *Christians at Work* Annual Conference.

39. Write an article about your CF group at work, and/or send a group photograph, for use in a future issue of *net.working.*

SPREADING INFORMATION

40. Prepare a single–page newsletter about your CF's aims and activities, and send it to evangelically minded churches in your area, asking for their prayer support.

41. Produce a newsletter, every six months, on two sides of A4, folded (four sides of A5), about your CF at work, and distribute it to colleagues. The content could include your CF programme, a testimony, and news of past and coming activities.

MISCELLANEOUS

42. If you have local pastors as CF speakers, offer them a conducted tour of the site (if practicable), to increase their familiarity with the working world. This will help their ministry, and improve their awareness of your group's circumstances and witness.

43. If your company sponsors students who work for part of the year at your workplace, invite them to CF meetings, and befriend them, whether or not they are Christians. Keep in touch by letter while they are at university or college.

44. If you have the equipment and the skill, make a good–quality amateur video or DVD of the testimony of one of your CF members, linking working life with Christian faith and experience. Such videos could be made available to other CF groups in workplaces.

11

TOWN CENTRE GROUPS

Most of the Christian Fellowship groups affiliated to *Christians at Work* exist in single workplaces and are made up of Christians who work for the same employer. From experience over the years, we regard this as the ideal arrangement, for reasons outlined below. However there are circumstances in which it is more practicable for CF groups to exist which meet in a neutral venue and are made up of Christians who work for different employers. Such groups are most likely to exist in town or city centres or on industrial estates.

Compared with groups in single workplaces, a town centre group suffers from a number of disadvantages. But there are also some advantages, and some specific opportunities to be an effective force for good.

In the interests of brevity, the expression 'town centre group' has been used throughout this chapter. Nonetheless, the same principles and suggestions are also applicable to a group of Christians who might be employed, for example, on an industrial estate or in a large out–of–town shopping complex.

SOME ADVANTAGES AND DISADVANTAGES OF A TOWN CENTRE GROUP

The main disadvantages are as follows:

1. Because those involved work for different employers, there is not the sense of common identity or 'belonging' which is experienced by groups in single workplaces. This makes any kind of corporate activity or witness more difficult to target towards any particular group of people.

If having a CF group that might meet in its own workplace is something that does not seem relevant to many of the workforce, what chance has a meeting that is to be held five minutes' walk away?

2. A neutral venue, such as a church hall or a hotel function room, is bound to be a little distance away from local workplaces, making it less likely that non–Christian colleagues will be either able or willing to attend.

There is also a greater psychological barrier. Work colleagues will find a meeting in a church hall more intimidating than one held in a conference room within their own office premises.

The main advantage is that, by holding the meeting in a neutral venue, the gathering is opened up to a wider range of people who could potentially be invited, unhindered by the security restrictions which would inevitably inhibit access by outsiders to meetings held within a single workplace.

Moreover, there are obviously many places of work where there are just not enough Christians to start a CF group, and so a town centre group can, in such circumstances, make possible the formation of a viable group.

In any situation where there are both advantages and disadvantages, the important requirement is to build on the opportunities presented, and then to minimise the adverse effects of the hindrances.

A PROGRAMME FOR ACTION

In order to formulate clear aims, and to create a programme of activity and action that will fulfil those aims, the following questions should be considered:

1. For whom are the meetings of the town centre group intended?

The meetings can be aimed at all Christians working within easy reach of the chosen available venue, and also at the non–Christian colleagues of those Christians, who could be invited personally. Other people, such as retired people, would of course be welcome to attend, but it should always be remembered for whom the meetings are fundamentally intended.

There is a danger of town centre meetings gradually drifting into the style and content preferred by those who attend regularly, rather than the programme and arrangements being the result of a clear and prayerfully–considered aim and plan.

The evangelistic potential of meetings should always be borne in mind, as it will be self–defeating to become a 'holy huddle'. However, meeting content need not always be directly evangelistic. If the meetings convey truth about the Christian message and faith, then any non–Christians present will be having their ignorance replaced with knowledge, and they will be challenged to go on seeking.

2. What sort of meeting content would be most suitable for the people towards whom the meeting programme is aimed?

The most suitable programme is one that addresses, from a Christian and biblical perspective, themes and subjects of importance and interest both to Christians and non–Christians. Some topics might be more geared for Christians, and other topics more for non–Christians.

The programme could include: seasonal meetings; questions about Christianity; talks on 'my faith and my work'; or topics such as money, work and stress.

'Midweek in Mayfair' is a very successful town centre meeting which regularly attracts between fifty and sixty people from the Mayfair district of London. They have around four regular speakers and work out their programme on the basis of three 'terms' per year.

A series for Christians could look something like this:

Title: 'The Bottom Line'
Excellence — Genesis 1:26–31
Integrity — Psalm 26
Ambition — Philippians 2:10–13
Competition — Matthew 20:17–28
Profits — Ecclesiastes 5:4, etc.
Honesty — Ephesians 4:17–30
Respect — Ephesians 5
Fairness — Deuteronomy 10
Whistle–blowing — Matthew 18
Accountability — Romans 14

Rewards — Matthew 20:1–16
Commitments — Luke 14:15–35
Choices — Deuteronomy 30:11–20

Here is an example of a series with a more evangelistic focus:

Title: 'Can Life Make Sense?'
Hectic, but hollow — Ecclesiastes 1:1–18
Enjoy yourself, and then? — Ecclesiastes 2:1–17
Daily toil and restless nights — Ecclesiastes 2:18–26
There is a time for everything — Ecclesiastes 3:1–11
The 'God–shaped gap' inside — Ecclesiastes 3:10 –15
Better off dead? — Ecclesiastes 3:16–4:4
Rather fear God — Ecclesiastes 5:1–7
Why money can't satisfy — Ecclesiastes 5:10–17
How to enjoy what you have — Ecclesiastes 5:18–6:6
The laughter of fools — Ecclesiastes 7:1–10
Life's a mystery — Ecclesiastes 7:23–8:4
Is life like a lottery? — Ecclesiastes 9:1–12
Folly in high places — Ecclesiastes 10:12–18
God will bring you to judgement — Ecclesiastes 11:1–10
Remember your Creator — Ecclesiastes 12:1–14

The subjects included in each of those specimen programmes are, of course, just examples of a vast variety of topical subjects which might be selected.

As to the format of the meeting, inviting a suitable visiting speaker is a good approach, as this will be slightly more formal and less intimidating for a non–Christian colleague than a discussion–based, or 'sharing' style, meeting.

Non–Christians need to feel 'safe' and unthreatened, and this will be achieved if the focus and emphasis is on the advertised subject, rather than on the individual people attending the meeting.

You might also want to think about having (carefully chosen) people assigned to be available to pray with individuals after the meeting. There might be specific issues that need to be followed up. It would be good to have a small side room allocated for this purpose.

3. Are there any points that particularly need to be borne in mind in making the arrangements for a lunchtime town centre meeting?

Try to provide a hot drink to serve before the meeting. Not only is this welcome in itself, but it makes it easier for people to talk to one another while waiting for the meeting to start.

Plan for meetings to be reasonably short — say half an hour, maybe from 1.15 p.m. to 1.45 p.m., with tea and coffee served from 1.00 p.m. People are more likely to attend a short meeting than a longer one. Meetings must start and finish promptly as this will give people the confidence to trust the arrangements and to return to another meeting.

4. How widely are the meetings to be publicised, and by what means?

Meetings held in a neutral venue can be advertised very widely, but do keep in mind the practicalities of attendance within a limited lunch hour.

Offices within half a mile of the venue could be circulated, receptionists or personnel staff being asked to display advertisements on notice boards. Churches in the area could also be informed, but be careful not to let one church be over–influential.

Printed notices or programme cards could be produced,

and either mailed or delivered personally, along with explanatory letters. The most effective publicity, however, will be by word of mouth and personal invitation.

5. What other aims and goals can and should the town centre group have in view?

The group should always have in mind the setting–up of CF groups or small prayer groups in nearby single workplaces. Perhaps three or four Christians who all work in the same office block will start attending the town centre meeting. The idea of a small group starting up in that workplace could be made a target and a prayer topic.

It might be that a number of small cells or prayer groups could be set up, with everyone coming together for the main meeting. In other words, prayer could take place in small groups, and teaching could take place in the larger meeting.

12

PRAYER: LIFEBLOOD FOR THE WORKPLACE

There is a growing conviction amongst God's people that he is calling his church to prayer, and if the church will heed this call then there are great blessings in store.

> "If my people, who are called by my name, will humble themselves and pray and seek my face and turn from their wicked ways, then will I hear from heaven and will forgive their sin and will heal their land."
>
> *2 Chronicles 7:14*

Fom the very beginning, God and man conversed. God spoke to Adam and Eve, and they spoke to him. The heart of prayer is precisely that conversation —communication between man and God. As early as Genesis 4:26, we read that, '...at that time men began to call on the name of the Lord.'

Whether at home, work or church, we are powerless without prayer. Jesus said, "...apart from me you can do nothing" (John 15:5b). Paul wrote, 'I can do everything through him who gives me strength' (Philippians 4:13). James reassures us concerning prayer, writing, 'The prayer of a righteous man is powerful and effective' (James 5:16b).

Next to salvation itself, the ability to pray is the most powerful gift that God bestows upon his people at conversion; indeed, that gift is a fruit of salvation. We are given access by faith into the presence of the living God, and this enables us both to worship him aright and also to see him work when we pray —in places where he might not otherwise work. Prayer, therefore, is the fruit of the life-giving work of the Holy Spirit operating in the believer. Prayer brings spiritual stability and puts our lives into an inclusive perspective, in the sense that we are made aware of the amazing power of God —and of all that he has done for us and will do, through his Son, our Saviour, the Lord Jesus Christ.

SO, WHY PRAY CONCERNING OUR WORKPLACE?

Prayer reflects our relationship and response to God, and through prayer we must praise him and thank him for who he is.

Remember, before you pray together, it is important to spend a few moments in quiet personal prayer, to ensure that your relationship with God and one another is as it should be. So prepare your heart and confess any sin; it takes only one person, one member of the group who is out of fellowship with God, to spoil the effectiveness of your prayer time!

1. For ourselves....

When we consider our own situations in our workplaces, we become aware of our utter dependency upon the Lord Jesus

Christ. Work is the place where we are most likely to be at our weakest in faith. Our spiritual weakness, our sinful tendencies, can so often been seen 'at work'; and our faithful witness and our spiritual wellbeing depend upon our daily relationship with God through prayer. So we must pray for our daily walk with the Lord to be faithful and honouring to him —in our work, as in all aspects of our lives.

2. For the Holy Spirit....

We can do nothing in our own strength. We read in Zechariah 12:10 of how God pours out 'a spirit of grace and supplication' on his people. And Paul reminds us that we should 'pray in the Spirit on all occasions.' (See Ephesians 6:18.) The Holy Spirit is the giver of life, and we must pray for him to enter every situation of our lives —especially at work. If we are praying for those around us who need to be brought to faith in our Lord Jesus Christ, then in our prayers we must remember what Jesus said about the Holy Spirit: 'When he comes, he will convict the world of guilt in regard to sin and righteousness and judgment....' (John 16:8.)

3. For love....

God is continually revealing his own unique and special love for us. His love is beyond human understanding, because it is selfless; it perfectly forgives and forgets. It allows us to be treated by him as if we had never sinned. This love that has been poured out into our hearts should now be poured out for those around us —especially at work. At work we often see a side to people that we would never see outside work: confidences are shared; many things happen at work. Circumstances change at work; people have to meet crisis head on, and it is the faithful prayer of the Lord's people that will help sustain your colleagues through times of difficulty and stress. To pray is the very best we can do for them.

4. For the sake of our visible witness....

Work can be a place filled with temptation.

- To conform to the world's standards and live below our privileged life.
- To be dishonest, whether through indirect company policy or petty theft.
- To act in an immoral and spiritually unacceptable manner.
- To blank off our 'at work' conscience and to justify wrong actions.
- To speak, think, do and participate in things that would bring the Lord's name into disrepute and ruin your testimony.

It is vital that we are seen by those around us, including those with whom we work, as those who echo forth the truth from the platform of a changed life. We sustain this attitude and grow in Christlikeness by our daily communion with God, reading his word and praying constantly. Our testimony at work is the first and vital link in the chain. Our prayers constantly sustain this as a living reality, for ourselves and those with whom we seek to witness.

5. For our Saviour....

This is the most important reason for us to be faithful in prayer: 'But God demonstrates his own love for us in this: While we were still sinners, Christ died for us' (Romans 5:8). As the Lord's people, we are entrusted with a great task as messengers of the gospel. Our first function is to seek to draw people to a saving knowledge of Christ: in response to his vicarious death on the cross for our sins; in response to God's demonstration of his own love for each one of us. We must pray for those with whom we work; we must pray for opportunities to befriend them and gain their confidence; and we must pray that we might, through our witness at work, have the opportunity to present the gospel to a needy people. Prayer will open doors of opportunity.

6. Because of the activity of the devil....

We need protection from evil influence; we read in the Lord's Prayer: '...lead us not into temptation, but deliver us from the evil one.' The strategy of the devil—Satan—is no different from what it was in the Garden of Eden: he wants to separate us from God. He knows that he cannot take away our salvation but, if we let him, he can ruin our testimony, drawing us out of witness. We must pray—as the Lord Jesus Christ prayed for us in John 17—that the Father would protect us from evil. That should be our prayer every day, both corporately and individually. 'Watch and pray so that you will not fall into temptation. The spirit is willing, but the body is weak' (Matthew 26:41).

HOW, WHERE AND WHEN SHOULD WE PRAY?

The Bible is very clear about our prayer life. What it teaches is that we can pray at any time, any place, anywhere. The Psalmist cried out to God in the morning, noontime and evening, when in distress (see Psalm 55:17); but this reflects a good habit of regular prayer, for he also writes, 'Seven times a day I praise you...' (Psalm 119:164a). But when two or three (or more) Christians are gathered to pray, then prayer is much more powerful, because we have the presence of the Lord Jesus Christ with us in a special way, according to his promise. And when two or three agree in prayer then we see God work in his awesome power.

It is vital to pray together as a group in the workplace in obedient response to the commands and promises of God. Often, when this happens, more of the mighty potential of the power of God is evident in the situation for which you are praying.

Prayer should always be a priority in our lives. Jesus told his disciples the parable of the persistent widow, to show them that they should always pray and not give up. (See Luke 18:1).

We should pray until something happens –PUSH!

WHO AND WHAT DO WE SPECIFICALLY PRAY FOR?

- We should firstly always praise and worship God for who he is, and for putting us where we are.

- We should offer thanksgiving for our fellowship together and for those individuals who form the group (if we are in a group).

- We should pray also for other Christians in the workplace, who, for various reasons, may choose not to join in fellowship at work.

- Remember to pray for the people with whom you work.

- Pray for the company or organisation, for its integrity and for its success. There is no scripture that condemns the honest creation of wealth.

- Pray for those who have authority over you, for the management and directors.

- Remember to pray for your own witness, for profitable friendships, and for opportunity.

- Pray for one another for your needs and for your relationship with God.

As Warren Wiersbie has put it, when churches ('called out people') pray, God opens doors. When the Holy Spirit opens doors — opening minds, eyes and hearts — then Christians can do exciting things for God, to his glory.

13

A CHRISTIAN RESPONSE TO INDUSTRIAL ACTION

A change in the attitudes of employers and employees in recent years, backed up by a steady stream of legislation, has significantly reduced the number of damaging strikes taking place in the UK.

In spite of this, industrial disputes are still a frequent occurrence, though out of the spotlight of widespread press and media attention. Most disputes are local, short–lived and over minor issues, and do not involve strike action.

Each new dispute, however isolated and unpublicised, has the potential to present Christians employed in the affected workplaces with a dilemma over the attitude they should take when their section or department is suddenly embroiled in an employer–employee conflict.

This chapter examines some principles which can guide the Christian to a thought out, biblically consistent stance on issues which may arise. It poses a number of main questions, breaks down some of them into subsidiaries suitable for study or discussion, and suggests some answers.

A study of the issues will be a help to every employed Christian, whether on the shop floor or in the professional world. It may well prove easier to consider them now, in a general way, detached from any particular dispute, since there is little enough time to think things through after a dispute has suddenly begun.

1. How am I to judge the merits of the issue which has led to the dispute and resulting industrial action?

Objectively. Most people in the UK tend to believe either that the management is always right, or that the workforce is always right. This is because everyone (Christians included) is to some extent affected by his/her background. We need to guard against this, carefully finding out the facts and judging the issues on them, before lining up on either or neither side of a dispute.

Frequently. When a dispute first arises, the Christian has much to consider and pray over —but not only then. Disputes do not remain constant. Issues can change. Desired results can change. Tactics can change. A Christian needs to apply biblical principles to the changes which occur, and to be wary of too great a commitment to first impressions. A frequent review will be needed of what the dispute is currently about, and of the tactics being used by both sides.

On the basis of Scripture. Having established the facts, the Christian should look for, and examine closely, any Scriptures relevant to the issues at stake in the dispute, using the principles they advance to help form sound judgements on them.

For instance, if, to maximise his own advantages, the employer has broken a promise which he was able to meet, but has failed to fulfil, there is a principle in James 5:4 which touches on this:

Look! The wages you failed to pay the workmen who

> mowed your fields are crying out against you. The cries of the harvesters have reached the ears of the Lord Almighty.

If the dispute is over the refusal of a reasonable request for a change in working practices, there is a principle in Ephesians 6:5–8 which applies:

> Slaves, obey your earthly masters with respect and fear, and with sincerity of heart, just as you would obey Christ. Obey them not only to win their favour when their eye is on you, but like slaves of Christ, doing the will of God from your heart. Serve wholeheartedly, as if you were serving the Lord, not men, because you know that the Lord will reward everyone for whatever good he does, whether he is slave or free.

If the issue is about the vexed question of differentials, there are principles in Matthew 20:1–15 which relate to that.

These passages do not tell us whether or not we should go on strike. They help us to judge the case presented on either side. They assist us in understanding God's view of the issues, so that we can adopt the same view as he does. The Bible is not an industrial relations manual, but as we find out what pleases God, we will be better equipped to steer a faithful course through disputes which may arise in our workplace.

2. How does industrial action fit with a Christian understanding of what work is?

The Bible strongly advocates work as part of the normal Christian life, and gives several reasons for this which include:

- Work makes good use of our talents and abilities. (See Matthew 25:15f; Titus 3:14).

- Work is the means by which we are enabled to provide for ourselves, our families, and others in need. (See Ephesians 4:28; 1 Timothy 5:8; Titus 3:14).

- Work is a discipline against idleness and its harmful effects. (2 Thessalonians 3:6, 12).

How, if at all, would these principles be threatened by our involvement in the various kinds of industrial action open to an employee?

3. Where do my loyalties lie?

In connection with industrial disputes, different valid loyalties may appear to collide. In determining our own actions, how are we to evaluate our loyalty to God, to our family, to our employer, to our colleagues, and to fellow-Christians? What are the essential ingredients of these differing loyalties, and where do the collisions occur? In a dispute, can all these loyalties be reconciled? Will the honouring of our loyalty to God, once we know where that lies, fulfil all our other real loyalties also?

(a) Loyalty to God

Paul wrote: 'So whether you eat or drink or whatever you do, do it all for the glory of God' (1 Corinthians 10:31). If we are to be faithful to the words of Scripture, then we have to ask ourselves the question: would industrial action bring glory to God?

(b) Loyalty to our employer

It is impossible to go on strike without breaching an employment contract. Is an employer one of those meant by Romans 13:7, 'Give everyone what you owe him: If you owe taxes, pay taxes; if revenue, then revenue; if respect, then respect; if honour, then honour.' These words are powerful. Is breaching a contract a denial of a Christian's word or promise —a failure to, "let your 'Yes' be 'Yes'"? (See Matthew 5:37)? If this is to be interpreted in this absolute and faithful way, then **no Christian should ever go on strike.** This point is a serious one.

Or can the 'breach of contract' dilemma be answered by an argument that circumstances are no longer the same as those on which the contract was based, but have been changed unilaterally by the employer, thus causing the dispute?

Is the 'balance of evils' argument viable in these circumstances? This is a perilous calculation for fallen man to make, but are there ever circumstances in which a Christian can break a contract in order to help to rectify another evil, equally wrong in the sight of God? What priority should we give the 'balance of evils' argument, compared with the search for other ways, short of breaking a contract, of rectifying the injustice or evil?

Peter writes,

> Slaves, submit yourselves to your masters with all respect, not only to those who are good and considerate, but also to those who are harsh. For it is commendable if a man bears up under the pain of unjust suffering because he is conscious of God.
>
> *1 Peter 2:18–19*

(c) Loyalty and the local church

In a small town, any major industrial dispute will be front page news in the local press, and those working at the company or authority affected will be in the public eye. In these circumstances it would be most helpful for the Christian involved in an industrial dispute to inform his or her church leaders about it, and to listen to any advice they are able to offer. If the details can be explained to the whole church by the church officers, it would result not only in better understanding, but prayer, sympathy, and encouragement for the fellow–member.

4. How will involvement in industrial action affect my witness?

One definition of Christian witness might be **commending Christ by life and word**. By this definition, witness occurs every day, and involves both what we do and what we say. But it is not essentially about pleasing people or persuading them to agree with you. It is about commending Christ.

Christians need also to remember that they are not dictating to others, but seeking to order their own lives in the light of God's word. As Donald Guthrie has pointed out, although modern industry is not run on Christian principles, Christians are not absolved from the responsibility of acting on Christian principles.

The test of a Christian's witness is not whether people agree with his words and actions, but whether what he says and does commends the reality of his faith and testimony. The way we are viewed by people, and therefore our witness, is affected by three elements which are always important, but which are particularly relevant to the conduct of a Christian in an industrial dispute:

(a) The importance of communication

Can you explain to people in simple terms consistent with God's word why you are taking part, or not taking part, in industrial action? Be careful how you do this, for it is easy to appear strangely apologetic. When someone says, "I must take this line, because of what God says", it can easily seem as though they are saying, "I would not choose this path myself, but since I am a Christian and have to do what God says, I haven't any choice." This attitude is that of a reluctant follower, distancing himself from God. It betrays an empty legalism which carries no credibility whatever, and spoils witness. We do not only follow God's way because he says so, but because we believe he is right.

(b) The manner of your speaking

Is your conversational tone godly and restrained? Is it generous to those who hold the view with which you disagree? Christians are not good witnesses when they are polemical, bigoted or immoderate in their demeanour or speech, nor when they are poor listeners to other views.

(c) The need to avoid 'extremism'

Are you a balanced Christian? It is no part of a Christian's witness to draw attention to himself or herself by a display of self–righteousness, 'martyrdom', or conduct designed to shock others, or by trying to outdo colleagues in the degree of passion for the cause. A Christian's motives are as important as his conduct. He does not enter an industrial dispute in order to be a witness or to be influential. Nor does he opt out in order to be noticed.

5. Is an industrial dispute my responsibility, or just something I should go along with, and hope it is over soon?

God, in his providence, has his representatives in all kinds of situations. Consider Joseph, Moses, Obadiah (1 Kings 18), Nehemiah, Esther and Daniel. At times their environments, and the people around them, were hostile to their faith, but it was all in God's plan. They were a mixture of characters, some of them with noted weaknesses, but hardly any of them were negative or passive people.

The Christian cannot be unresponsive to his circumstances, but he does need to seek God's wisdom as to what can be said and done to please God, and fulfil his purposes, day by day. To speak and act appropriately may require courage, and almost always a blend of confidence and gentleness.

Once you have come to a view about the dispute, try to arrange to see your local union leader, and a representative of your local management, separately, to explain how you view the issues, and why you view them in that light. This could be reinforced by a follow–up letter to each of them. No Christian will come to harm through stating honest, thought–out views courteously and sincerely.

As human beings, have you noticed that when we are in difficulties, we have a tendency to react much faster than when life is something like normal? We should stop and reconsider, we should stop and regroup; oh, yes, of course, we can always stop to pray the problem through —that usually is the last thing we do! Where is faith at these times? And what about when we run ahead of God? According to Romans 1:17, 'The righteous will live by faith.' By grace, through faith, God brings us into his kingdom. When you read the life of Abraham in Genesis chapters twelve to twenty five, you see that what God did, he did to perfect Abraham's faith. Hebrews tells us much about the need for faith, and this is, in fact, a spiritual principle.

God works in and through our lives, giving us faith and using that faith. The thing that hinders the work of God on earth is never any lack of power in him — it is his people's lack of faith.

Do you remember the Lord's response to lack of faith? 'And he did not do many miracles there because of their lack of faith' (Matthew 13:58). But in Matthew 9:29b we read, "According to your faith will it be done to you."

This raises an important question: How can we know that we are living by faith? It is so easy for us to be fooled by our own feelings or by the circumstances around us, or even by Satan and his demonic powers. So what are the tests that we can apply to our actions and decisions?

How do we know that we are walking by faith?

There is one key, simple test. **Ask yourself: Am I doing this for the glory of God, or just to please myself?**

Paul wrote concerning Abraham:

> Yet he did not waver through unbelief regarding the promise of God, but was strengthened in his faith and gave glory to God....
>
> *Romans 4:20*

Abraham and Sarah were both old, and certainly past their child–bearing and rearing years, when God promised them a son. ***Nothing is impossible with God!*** F.B. Meyer reminded us that we never really trust God until we trust him to do the impossible!

Abraham and Sarah producing a child in their very old age was impossible apart from God. It was not Abraham's faith in faith that brought about the miracle; it was his faith in God! The world's shallow philosophy, *'Have faith–everything will work out'*, is as foolish as it is ineffective. Faith in what? Certainly not faith in faith! Abraham and Sarah trusted God, and God performed what he had promised.

Because he knew God, Abraham was, '...fully persuaded that God had power to do what he had promised.' (See Romans 4:21).

What it is important for you and I to realise is that Abraham's motive in all of this was to give all the glory to God. Faith always gives glory to God, because faith acknowledges and confirms that man is unable to accomplish anything, and that only God can do it.

So as you make your decision, ask yourself the question in your Christian witness or service: **Is it to—or for—the glory of God?** If it is not, then stand back and wait.

If there is a thought in your heart and mind that what you are doing or saying is out of selfishness or self glory, STOP IMMEDIATELY! **True faith is only ever motivated by the desire to glorify God!**

14

MEETING THE NEEDS OF THE WORKING CONGREGATION

Being on the mission field is a full–time occupation involving time stress, people pressure and spiritual warfare. Almost every missionary or missionary group has their own backup group, which supports them in prayer and financially.

If this is the support structure for full–time Christian workers, what can the church provide for those who spend 37.5 hours or more on the front lines at work, and then come home to face family and church demands?

Is a full–time career or vocation a sort of second–class occupation, compared to the work of full–time missionaries? Certainly not, for the fact is that God provides opportunities to share the gospel in the ordinary workplace, just as he does in the mission field of the classic missionary. What matters is that you are obedient to him in your own particular calling —which means actively looking out for those God–given opportunities.

We seek here to give some practical ideas about how the local church can provide the same kind of support to those in full–time jobs as it does to full–time missionaries.

There are some churches where most of the congregation are retired, and they can be encouraged both to support and pray for others in the world of employment, and to grow in their understanding that it is not only paid work which is of value. Many 'works' of love and mercy which stemmed from faith and compassion are shown and approved in the Bible. The work of caring for others in practical ways was demonstrated repeatedly in the earthly ministry of Jesus, and its value affirmed as he received hospitality and other acts of caring from those who loved him. Unpaid work is real work in the kingdom, no matter how often it is unrecognized by the world!

But a proportion of most congregations will be engaged in formal work situations of one sort or another, whether paid or voluntary, and their needs can and should be addressed.

SERMONS

Ministers and others who preach and teach in local churches should be providing real help and support by way of sermons which are in touch with today's work environment. Such sermons can be arranged as an annual series over several weeks, or at other convenient intervals.

It is helpful to include examples from life in the workplace when applying the main principles from a passage.

Material can be obtained from:

- The *Christians at Work* website or resource index, which includes *Christians at Work* briefing papers, articles from various publications, historical and contemporary books, etc.

- Adapting Bible studies. *Christians at Work* produces short Bible studies in three series, which can be used in the preparation of sermons. There are also a number of other Bible study series listed on the website.

- Cassette tapes. 'Midweek in Mayfair' produce a catalogue of lunchtime talks which can be used as the basis of a sermon. *Christians at Work* Annual Conference tapes can also be used. Ian Coffey has produced a series of morning sermons on cassette and these are available from Mutley Baptist Church (address at the end of this chapter).

PASTORAL CARE

Pastoral care, whether carried out in house groups, pastorates or other small groups (of which more below), or by personal contact by the minister or a team of pastoral assistants, or in a combination of these and other ways, needs to be marked by an awareness of the needs of working people. Some ways to encourage and help the working population in your congregation are:

- To invite prayer requests relating to the workplace for inclusion on your pastoral list.

- Provide home visits for the unemployed, or those with bigger problems at work.

- Pray in the main church services for people witnessing at work, as often as you do for missionaries serving overseas. Why not target each month a particular employment sector —such as teachers, engineers, care workers, factory workers, service providers, medical staff, etc.

- Be sure that you do not put pressure on people to get so involved in organisational 'church' activities, responsibilities and functions that they have no time for family and friends, and witnessing outside of work to colleagues.

- Especially if you are a church leader (minister, elder, lay preacher, etc.): You have many calls on your time, but *make* time to listen to Christians who are willing to talk about their working lives and the challenges and opportunities they face in the light of their faith.

MONEY MATTERS

Most churches will give some attention to the necessity for faithful, generous giving, and many teach the biblical principles relating to that. More people can be encouraged to give according to biblical guidelines, and there may be opportunities to affirm faithfulness and obedience in this area. It can sometimes be helpful to focus on the links between work, money as the reward for many kinds of work, and our giving as the response to the amazing generosity of our Creator God and the capacity he has given us to work and so to earn money. There must of course be sensitivity towards those who are not themselves in paid employment, and, again, the value of unremunerated kinds of work (voluntary work, homemaking) must never go unrecognized.

EVENTS AND SEMINARS

Annually, or on a more frequent basis, evening or weekend events or seminars can be held to encourage people to keep thinking about their witness at work. *Christians at Work* is just one of the UK based organisations that will provide a speaker to run seminars. Others include the following, contact details for which will be found at the end of this book:

The London Institute of Contemporary Christianity (LICC)
Christian Viewpoint for Men (CVM)
International Christian Chamber of Commerce (ICCC)
Midweek in Mayfair
Ridley Hall (Richard Higginson)
Worknet Partnership
God at Work (Ian Coffey, Mutley Baptist)
Dr. David Kellett
Robin Scurlock

Saturday morning sessions can be built around a video or Bible study series by one of your own church members or from: LICC Videos, God at Work, and Christian Life and Work Mutley Baptist 'Christians in the Workplace' Breakfast Series, and Bible studies.

BIBLE STUDY

There are many Bible study series now available on work. The *Christians at Work* website lists a number of them. *Christians at Work* has produced three series of shorter Bible studies, which are designed for lunchtime meetings but leave the option for extended prayer time for specific issues at work in normal meetings.

SMALL GROUPS

Most churches have already acknowledged that effective teaching and pastoral cover cannot be achieved without the aid of small group activity, such as pastoral committees, luncheon clubs, prayer groups, Bible study groups, fellowship groups, etc. The small group network in your church may benefit from focusing a series of meetings on work–based issues.

These small groups can provide the individual prayer support on a regular basis that is not possible for a pastor alone—or even a pastoral team—to provide. Put workplace issues at the top of the prayer list for a while, and encourage the elderly prayer warriors to find out what those who have not yet retired are struggling with in today's work environment.

DAYTIME MEETINGS

Luncheon clubs and 'mums and tots' groups need not be left out. Why not invite a speaker to a luncheon club to explain how the older folk can help those at work through encouragement and prayer? Improve communication by comparing the different pressures that there are now with those encountered in the last century. Mothers face a whole different set of work pressures and joys. Study and discussion on how God values child care and family building, and how that fits in with the pressure to work, will help put things in perspective.

EVANGELISM

Whilst discipleship and attention to pastoral issues are essential to maintain the spiritual health and effectiveness of our Christian workforce, the main ministry at work is to witness for Christ —both 'one to one' and through prayer.

This personal witness can be enhanced by evangelism events. The network of *Christians at Work* fellowships put on various evangelism events in their companies.

The Church can help in two ways: prayer — e.g. prayer triplets, to focus on praying for specific colleagues at work; and holding evangelism events that would appeal to local workers and local businesses.

Here are some organisations which provide outreach seminars suitable for the local community (contact details on pages 126–128, together with those of some other organizations and people who can help in a variety of other ways):

SALT — on dealing with stress;
Credit Action — on money management;
ICCC — on management techniques for local businesses.

RESOURCES

There is an increasing amount of resource material available for Christian discipleship specific to work. It can be helpful to promote and make available these resources, since people do not automatically think of it themselves.

The *Christians at Work* website gives a comprehensive list of resources available, and offers links to other appropriate sites. If you do not have access to the internet, the *Christians at Work* office can send you information by post.

USEFUL CONTACT DETAILS

Christians at Work
PO Box 1746, Rugby CV21 3ZS
Tel. 01788 579738
Email: office@christiansatwork.org.uk
www.christiansatwork.org.uk

Christian Viewpoint for Men
Richard Meryon
Isabella House, The Avenue, Combe Down, Bath BA2 5EH
Tel. 01225 833748
Email: admin@cvmen.org.uk www.cvmen.org.uk

Credit Action
Howard House, The Point,
Weaver Road, Lincoln LN6 3QN
Tel. 01522 699777
Email: office@creditaction.org.uk www.creditaction.org.uk

ICCC
(Council of Christians in Commerce Ltd)
79–81 Newfoundland Street, Bristol BS2 9AP
Tel. 0117 924 9754 Fax 0117 924 9768
Email: office@uk.iccc.net www.uk.iccc.net

Dr. David Kellett
(Author of *Champions for God at Work*)
3 Lakeside, Wallington, Surrey SM6 7JY
Tel. 020 8773 3700
Email: davidkellett@Tiscali.co.uk

The London Institute for Contemporary Christianity (LICC)
St Peter's Church, Vere Street, London W1G 0DQ
Tel. 020 73 999 555 Fax 020 73 999 556
Email: mail@licc.org.uk www.licc.org.uk

Midweek in Mayfair
26 Binney Street, London W1Y 1YN
Tel. 020 7629 2348 Fax 020 7629 6480
Email: peter.matthew@midweek.org.uk

Mutley Baptist Church
Mutley Plain, Plymouth, Devon PL4 6LB
Tel. 01752 203346
Email: office@mutley–baptist.co.uk

Ridley Hall Foundation
Director: Richard Higginson
(and co–editor, Faith in Business Quarterly)
Ridley Hall, Cambridge CB3 9HG
Email: rah41@cam.ac.uk

Stress and Life Trust (SALT)
The Istana, Freezeland Lane
Bexhill–on–Sea, East Sussex TN39 5JD
Tel. 01424 219133

WorkNet
Contact Geoff Shattock, National Director
56 Baldry Gardens, London SW16 3DJ
Tel. 020 8764 8080
Email: info@worknetuk.org www.worknetuk.org

See also: www.worktalk.org.uk
for WorkTalk, a seven–part audio and handbook course on working well by working spiritually.

Robin Scurlock and Steve Goss
Authors of *I Love My Work* —a study book designed to help Christians develop a stronger biblical understanding of God's interest in and desire to be involved in their work lives wherever he has called them to work. It concentrates on the practical issues, pressures and questions faced every day in the workplace. Robin has a business background in the international telecoms industry and Steve leads *Freedom in Christ Ministries* in the UK.

For further information on this book, other faith/work–related resources and speaker availability for services, seminars, workshops and conferences, please contact:
www.ilovemywork.co.uk
or Robin Scurlock on 0118 979 4696